THE NEGRO AND THE DRAMA

BY

FREDERICK W. BOND

THE NEGRO AND THE DRAMA

*The Direct and Indirect Contribution Which the
American Negro Has Made to Drama and
the Legitimate Stage, with the
Underlying Conditions
Responsible*

By

FREDERICK W. BOND

McGrath Publishing Company
College Park, Maryland

Reprint McGrath Publishing Company 1969
Reprinted from the copy at Yale University Library
Library of Congress Catalog Card Number: 76-84103

Manufactured in the United States of America
by Arno Press, Inc., New York

The Negro and The Drama

CONTENTS

INTRODUCTION

American Negro drama is comparatively new— hardly a century old. It was not until after 1820 that it began to show signs of vigor in minstrel melodrama. Except for scattered examples, the Negro stage was in general disrepute with the more intelligent public and hardly considered by critics and other people of letters. In the last decade of that century, musical comedy, in the hands of a few trained Negroes, virtually displaced the minstrel shows. The efforts and influences of the versatile Negroes, together with assistance from white producers and a rising number of Negro actors, resulted in a better type of drama. But it was not until O'Neill, Green, Leslie, and Belasco became interested in the Negro as thematic material that the merit of Negro drama was established.

The attention of these playwrights has been absorbed in the Negro's background which has been a continuous life of drama. Much of this tragic and comic entertainment, dealing directly and indirectly with Afro-Americans, is traced to the fact that the Negro can easily throw off inhibitions. The white producers and playwrights have commercialized his art.

The problem. The problem in this study is threefold: (1) To determine the elements which motivated and inspired the American Negro to enter the field of drama as a profession; (2) to determine the American Negro's contribution to the drama and to the legitimate stage, with regard to such activities as acting, writing and producing plays; (3) to consider the other dramatic arts connected with and having a bearing on drama, such as folklore, mimicry, music, and dancing.

Procedure. The procedure in this study has involved the following steps: (1) An examination of dramatic literature, such as (a) journals of speech and dramatics, (b) dramatic studies made by and of Negroes, (c) dramatic contributions which Negroes have made to newspapers and periodicals, (d) dramatic critiques which have been contributed to books, journals, periodicals, pamphlets, and newspapers, (e) clippings which have been preserved in scrap-books by persons interested in this phase of Negro development, (f) programs and announcements of plays of Negro life and character; (2) an analysis of other sources, such as (a) literature from those who are, or have been, interested in the Negro's dramatic efforts, (b) information received from little theatres and schools, (c) photostatic copies of primary data, (d) information received through personal letters.

Method of handling data. Inasmuch as the writer proposed to develop these data in historical sequence, he has presented a chronological discussion of that phase of drama which the Negro has been instrumental in producing. After briefly considering the cultural, economic, and social backgrounds which have directly and indirectly influenced Negro drama, the writer critically examined the better plays of the various periods. In a similar manner he has discussed the sponsors and producers of these plays.

Value of study. The value of this study lies in the following facts: (1) The subject of Negro drama has been treated only briefly in books, periodicals and newspapers, and this study is a systematic development of the Negro actor's rise from the shambles of minstrelsy to consciously artistic drama. (2) The study presents a survey of the best that has been done, by Negroes, in the entire field of drama.

Scope and limitations. The scope of this study is limited to the dramatic activities of the American Negro actor and actress in such branches of drama as writing, producing, singing, dancing and acting. Although the treatment has been confined to the dramatic role of the American Negro, nevertheless, wherever European exhibitions of the American Negro merit discussion such exhibitions have been discussed.

CHAPTER I

BACKGROUNDS OF NEGRO DRAMA

The idea that the American slave was intellectually and esthetically empty was discarded by the end of the nineteenth century. The culture of the Negro dates back to his African ancestry. The songs and literature which he produced in the seventeenth and eighteenth centuries were not the works of a group that lacked culture. These manifestations, sympathetically considered, must be classified as significant contributions to American culture.

The habits, customs, and emotions of the slaves were expressed in the form of songs. Through these natural compositions, the slaves in their naive manner compared temporal life with that of an eternal holiday in glory. Without these canticles, the slaves were bewildered and friendless. Their theme was "Trouble don't last always." Although many of these slave songs were saturated with religious fervor, others were, nevertheless, restricted to servile experiences, relying largely upon the slaves' imagination. These plantation songs had their source in the spontaneous surgings of religious intensity or in the discordant harshness of bondage. Though the words and language are often crude, and the strains wild, they are the outpourings of a group that has hardly been surpassed in this phase of music.[1] Even with the slaves' primi-

[1] Thomas P. Fenner, *Religious Folksongs of the Negro.* Hampton Institute, 1909, pp. iii-vi.

1

tive harmonies and limited vocabularies, they were able to portray life itself—that which came from the soil and the human soul. The Negro took as his basic material his native African rhythms and the King James version of the Bible, and out of them created the spirituals.[2]

These songs had their origin, for the most part, in the camp meetings, the revivals, and in other forms of religious activity. The slaves' whole-hearted faith in a personal Redeemer was true consolation. Moreover, they felt that ultimately they would pass out of bondage into a place of eternal comfort. That many of the words were taken literally out of the Bible and put into crude verses and stanzas is evident. The Bible was as basic in the composition of these songs as it was in that of the slaves' poetry; but the inspiration that caused the slaves to bring into play the swaying of the body, the stamping of the feet, and all the other emotional enthusiasms of the camp meeting, dates back to their African ancestry.[3]

The first Negro writer of any merit was Jupiter Hammon. He was born in 1730. He spent his life in slavery. His kind master taught him the three R's, and permitted him to attend church where, through constant reading of the Bible, he assimilated conceptions and impressions which greatly intensified his poetry. Moreover, he labored with Charles Wesley's hymns until he had such familiarity with them that his singing received compliments from various audiences.

[2] James W. Johnson, *Contribution of the Negro.* Unpublished Manuscript, New York University, 1937.
[3] M. Levison, *The Negro Dance Under European Eyes, The Theatre Arts Monthly,* May, 1927, pp. 282-287.

BACKGROUNDS OF NEGRO DRAMA

Despite its lack of literary merits the following poem is indicative of how much Hammon drew on the Bible:[4]

Salvation comes from the Lord
Salvation surely bring
Dear Jesus give the spirit now
That hasn't the Lord to whom we bow
The Author of salvation
Give us the preparation
We seen Thy true salvation.

Soon after Jupiter Hammon, there came upon the American scene during the 1770's a poet of more renown, Phyllis Wheatley.[5] Her biography leads one to assume that she was endowed with a talent that greatly influenced her writings. Though she wrote on various subjects, most of her writings had a religious tinge. Perhaps the most typical of her writings is the following:[6]

"Twas mercy brought me from my pagan land
Taught my benighted soul to understand
That there is a God, that there is a Saviour, too,
Once I redemption neither sought nor knew."

Phyllis Wheatley was a scholar of no little repute, if judged according to the standards of that day. She was steeped in the masterpieces of literature, of mythology, and Pope's Homer. It is reasonable to conclude that she was so influenced by the literary masters of England that she not only paraphrased them but followed their style. As for instance:[7]

[4] *Colored American*, Vol. 1, January 23, 1860, p. 3.
[5] Phyllis Wheatley, *Poems on Various Subjects*, 1816, p. 16.
[6] Vernon Loggins, *The Negro Author*, p. 2.
[7] *Colored American*, Vol. 1, January 23, 1838.

3

> While thus he spake the hero of renown
> Survey'd the boaster with a gloomy frown
> And stern replied "O arrogance of tongue
> Believ'st thou chief, that armies such as thine
> Can stretch in dust that heaven defended line."

Like many American writers of the period she considered the works of English writers as literary standards. A casual glance at any of her works will bring to light striking traces of John Milton, Alexander Pope, and other writers of the seventeenth and eighteenth centuries.

With all their merit, the works of Phyllis Wheatley are to be appreciated more on the ground of their efforts than from the point of view of their literary value. It is generally considered that most of her poems demonstrated little more than mediocre mastery and technique from the point of view of originality, material and depth. And yet there are several of her poems that may be considered for their Biblical influences and religious tint. It is regretted by many that Phyllis Wheatley neglected almost entirely to give her views concerning the oppression of her people. It was only when she addressed the poem to the Earl of Dartmouth, upon his appointment as secretary for North America, that she displayed her reactions regarding the oppression of slaves.

One especial feature of Phyllis Wheatley was that she was interested in problems of vital, present day interest. The occasion of the Stamp Act, the Declaration of Independence, the appointment of Washington as commander-in-chief of the Revolutionary forces, the betrayal of General Lee to the British foe, the victory of Washington—all came within the purview of

4

her observation.[8] Sometimes she wrote poems to console persons who had lost their friends and relatives.

After the poetic contributions of Phyllis Wheatley, who was at her height during the 1770's, little literary contribution came from Negroes until the appearance of George Moses Horton. The twenty poems published by Ann Plato of Hartford in 1841 are considered void of interest and lacking in imagination. Although J. M. Simpson, James Madison Bell, Frances Ellen Watkins Harper, and Charles L. Reason wrote during a later period, they did not excel Horton.

Indeed, Horton was probably the most distinguished poet between Wheatley and Dunbar. Horton's literary environment, however, was by no means as conducive to literary production as that of Phyllis Wheatley. He belonged to James Horton of Chatham County, North Carolina, who, having no personal culture himself, did not encourage productions of literature. Nevertheless, the Horton family was kindly and generous; and, as a consequence Horton's poetry found its way to the white press. For example, several of his pieces appeared in the Raleigh *Register;* some found their way to Boston, and others appeared freely in anti-slavery magazines and newspapers of both races. Working on the farm all day, he dictated his poems to others at night. Much of his feeling of depression is shown in the following short poem:[9]

> Come, melting pity, from afar
> And break the vast enormous bar
>   Between a wretch and thee
> Purchase a few short days of time,
> And bid a vassal soar sublime on
>   Wings of liberty.

[8] George M. Horton, *Poems by a Slave*, 1837, p. 2.
[9] *Ibid.*, p. 8.

5

In another poem, Horton appears more indignant at his plight, and expresses his feelings rather strongly. The fourth stanza from ''On Liberty and Slavery,'' is indicative of his emotions:[10]

> Roll through my ravished ears,
> Come let my grief in joys be drowned
> And drive away my fears.
> Say unto foul oppression cease
> Ye tyrants rage no more.

Perhaps the poem which evoked the greatest expressions of approbation was Horton's ''Praise of Creation.'' This attracted the attention of such men as Horace Greely, editor of the New York *Tribune,* and William Lloyd Garrison, editor of the *Liberator.* The stanza quoted below will give an insight into its character:[11]

> Creation fires my tongue
> Nature thy anthem raise
> And spread the universal song
> Of thy Creator's praise
> Heaven's chief delight was man
> Before creation's birth.

In music and poetry the Negro found his natural means of expression. There were, however, many Negroes, who had made contributions to prose before the close of the eighteenth century. Many motives inspired these efforts—such as the founding of the church, eulogies, fraternal organizations, and general acts of oppression.

One Negro who held claims of merit in the nineteenth century was Richard Allen, the first Negro bishop of America. His influence was confined prin-

[10] *Ibid.,* p. 3.
[11] G. F. Bragg, *Richard Allen and Absalom Jones,* Baltimore, Church Advocate Press, 1915, pp. 12-13.

cipally to the church, but his pastoral connections created in him a desire to write. The occasion for one of his first published utterances grew out of the ejection of Negroes from the St. George's Methodist Church in Philadelphia, in 1787, when the Negroes thus treated organized the ''Free African Society.''[12] In addition to his autobiography, Allen has to his credit another contribution to prose which gives an account of struggles against hardships—from the date of his birth,[13] to his triumph in the ministry. This work was his refutation of Matthew Carey's contention that, since Negroes were less susceptible to contagious disease than the whites, the former should have nursed the sick and buried the dead of the Philadelphia catastrophe of 1787. Allen was a man of intellectual, moral and spiritual preeminence, and a man whose views were eagerly sought on matters of importance.[14]

Richard Allen is taken, here, however, more as a type than as a sole contributor during his day. The prose works of Thomas Marrant, Nathaniel Paul, Peter Williams, and Theodore S. Wright, religious and anti-slavery workers, who survived Richard Allen were even more literary than those of the first Negro bishop, although not so important as beginnings of the Negro in literature.

When the thought expressed by the Negro became more anti-slavery than religious the popular writers were James Forten, William Whipper, Robert Purvis, J. W. C. Pennington, Samuel R. Ward, James Mc-

[12] *Ibid.*, p. 10.
[13] *Ibid.*, p. 8-11.
[14] Frederick Douglass, *Life and Times*, Boston, DeWolfe, Fisk and Co., 1892, pp. 418-419.

Cune Smith, Henry Highland Garnet, Charles Bennett Ray, David Ruggles, Charles Lenox Remond, and above all Frederick Douglass.

How voluminous were the writings of Douglass can never be known. His house burned down in 1872, destroying twelve volumes of his rarest papers, covering the period from 1840 to 1860.[15] His early contributions, therefore, cannot be accurately evaluated.

Douglass made a favorable impression in his first speech before the Anti-Slavery Convention assembled at Nantucket on August 11, 1841, but in the issue of Garrison's *Liberator* for November 18, 1842, appeared Douglass' first printed utterance. One George Litimer was held in a Boston jail as a fugitive slave. The cruelty of the whole idea was so provoking to Douglass that he wrote his reactions. The essay was characterized by such indignation that it caught the eye of Garrison; from then on the success of Douglass was assured. Beginning in this somewhat humble manner, Douglass found space in every abolition journal in the country.[16]

Despite the mediocrity of his early writings, which were crude and simple according to his own attestation, Douglass's works were soon to become well known. They are without doubt from the mind of one acquainted with literature of Whittier, the slave's poet, and with the oratory of the great leaders and spokesmen of the universe.

Of the many productions of Douglass nothing portrays his feeling more dramatically than his strong article, which appeared in the *North Star* at the outset of the Civil War. It runs thus:

[15] Frederick Douglass, *op. cit.*, p. 419.
[16] *Ibid.*, p. 415.

"Better even die free than to live slaves. This is the sentiment of every brave colored man amongst us. I have not thought lightly of the words I am now addressing you."[17]

In thus addressing the bondmen Douglass was not more radical than David Walker and Henry Highland Garnet, who had done the same in 1828 and 1843, respectively. The difference was that these forerunners spoke when to act on such advice would have meant suicide like that of Nat Turner in 1831.

Douglass's greatest contribution was his *Life and Times* of which George L. Ruffin wrote:

It is the greatest contribution, the author and subject of this book that has been introduced to the public. The contribution comes naturally and legitimately and to some not unexpectedly, nevertheless, it is altogether unique and must be regarded as truly remarkable. Our Pantheon contains many that are illustrious and worthy, but Douglass, he cannot be matched.[18]

The Negro in freedom passed through a period of exultation from the new boon of citizenship to a transition period to face again the ordeal of struggle. The deliberative oratory of Negro statesmen like J. H. Rainey, J. M. Langston, James T. Rapier, R. B. Elliott, and B. K. Bruce made a deep impression on the thoughtful citizenry, but the most dramatic production appeared in the writing of *Up From Slavery* by Booker T. Washington, who desired to lead the Negro toward practical achievement.

This story recounted how when working in a salt mine in West Virginia he overheard one of his fellow workers say that somewhere in Virginia was a school

[17] *Ibid.*, p. iv.
[18] Booker T. Washington, *Up From Slavery*. New York, Doubleday, Page and Co., 1900, pp. 42-51.

through which one could work his way. It was not long after hearing those remarks that he set out for Hampton Institute, resting his weary body beneath bridges when he became too tired to walk farther. In the same spirit he worked his way through that school. After being graduated from Hampton Institute, he went to Tuskegee, Alabama, where he built the largest Negro school of that type in the world. He became a personage of character, reputation, culture, and distinction, having dined with the royalty of Europe, and with Theodore Roosevelt then President of the United States.

Behind the recent contributions of the Negro in the drama lie certain economic and social forces of unusual significance. The census of 1930 listed 12,900,-000 Negroes that comprise the black population of the United States. Prior to the World War, over 75 per cent of the colored population resided in their native South—between Virginia and Texas where cotton flourished. During and immediately after that great conflict one million blacks migrated to the larger eastern cities to secure unskilled work. This movement reached its climax in the golden twenties, only to be abruptly stopped with the 1929 financial crash. Those stranded in the cities suffered much misery, having been pushed out of servile and menial toil. Their wealth, which had climbed from $20,000,000 at the close of the War between the states to $2,000,000,000[19] in 1926, was now in a tottering condition due to the economic depression.

For various reason the condition of the Negroes be-

---

[19] From figures compiled by Monroe H. Work, Director, Dept. of Records and Research, Tuskegee Institute for the *World Almanac*, 1936.

came discouraging. Less than a fourth of Negro farmers are owners. That, of course, means that a great majority of them are tenants.[20] In this respect they are not far removed from virtual slavery. The plantation owner, who is usually a white merchant, supplies the land and maintenance. The blacks furnish the labor.

Teaching, business, and industry are not sufficient to absorb the services of all Negroes. The average Negro high school teacher in the black belt receives less than $600.00 a year. The average elementary teacher receives $423.00.[21] In business the Negro has proved to be successful only in restaurants, barber shops, pool rooms and hairdressing—fields in which he does not have to compete with the white businesses. In the professions, college presidents, physicians, and ministers seem to surpass economically those in other activities.

Though figuratively free the Negro has remained in a state of economic servitude. The credit system together with other oppressive influences has vanquished him on every hand. Low wages have prevented his saving for periods of unemployment and depressions. Occupations to which he has been relegated have been few, servile, and of short duration.

In addition to the problem of earning a living the Negro has suffered immensely because of his violation of the statutes of his community. Living in slums and unhealthy environments, he has dwelt in the breeding beds of crime. Money that he might have used to ad-

[20] *World Almanac*, 1936, p. 260.
[21] G. S. Dow, *Society and Its Problems*, New York, Thomas Y. Crowel Co., 1929, pp. 198-199. See also C. S. Johnson, *A Preface to Racial Understanding*, New York, Friendship Press, 1936.

vantage elsewhere has had to be paid out for paltry infractions of the law.

In politics the race has not had success. Politically, the Negro has been responsible for his own failure. Though the Fifteenth Amendment to the Constitution enfranchised him, he has not used the ballot effectively. As a consequence, he has been kept out of public office, and other positions dependent upon votes.

Dow, exaggerating, observed that the rank and file of Negroes are shiftless, easygoing, docile, irresponsible, neurotic, and indifferent toward the future, going to and fro seeking sympathy and undeserved consideration.[22] After the World War, however, this condition of Negroes improved. Better educational opportunity had its effect. Pauperism, though greatly accentuated during the depression, steadily decreased after the 1880's. Yet, while reliable statistics are not available, it is variously stated by relief authorities of the larger cities throughout the country that two-thirds of those on relief today are Negroes. Discrimination, together with a dearth of jobs and positions, has been largely instrumental in forcing Negroes to seek charity. Where there has been a scarcity of work, with whites and blacks applying at the same time, the inherent tendency has been to accommodate those of the white race first. The belief is that the efficiency and reliability of the whites may be depended upon.[23]

In the religious field the Negro has had much opportunity, but he has not always used it effectively, as the number of ministers and their procedure show. Although the Negro may not faithfully practice Chris-

[22] G. S. Dow, *op. cit.*, pp. 198-199.
[23] *Ibid.*, p. 101.

12

tianity, he has ostensibly embraced this doctrine, and with a literalness of which we have not seen a parallel since the days of Jonathan Edwards. Having been forced to worship in separate churches, however, Negro preachers who did not come under the Catholic influence of Louisiana or that of the British possessions, had to piece out their discourse as best they could so that it would sermonize. Naturally, therefore, their scripture was based on the memory of what they had heard from "their white folks" whose familiarity with the Bible, too, needed serious mending. Their religion was handed down from generation to generation. Crude dialect came. Ira D. A. Reid, of the National Urban League, on making a study of Negro churches in Baltimore in 1935, was shocked to find such a large number of denominations, named after striking phrases of the Bible, such as, *The Holy Church of the Living God, Pillar and Ground of Truth, Prophet Bess, Church of the Temple of Love, and Church of the Divine Silence and Truth.*[24] Recent forms of religion which have made the most tremendous incursion into the Christian life of the colored population have been what are called the Holy Rollers, the Church of Christ, and the Father Divine Faith.

A most interesting exhibition may be observed in any of these so-called services. It is a sight to behold the worshipers jumping, prancing, crying, mourning, beating of instruments, shouting, wallowing on the dirt and sawdust floor, and wailing until the participants become exhausted, and are carried out in a state

[24] Ira De A. Reid, *The Negro Community of Baltimore*, the National Urban League, 1935, pp. 30-36.

of collapse. Exhortatory language, reminding the congregation of hell and damnation reverberate through the makeshift building from early Sunday morning till late Sunday night, to be followed successive nights during the week.[25] This religious fervor is only interspersed with pleas for money, to run "God's Work," taking the form of curt remarks and cajoling. The sermons need no playwrights or producers to revise or touch them up. Were it possible to lift them bodily to the stage in their original form, without the slightest bit of coloring, the audience would more than receive the worth of the admission fees. The sermons are profane, somewhat debasing, abusive, uncouth, vulgar, coarse and threadbare, and never omit, however, to lampoon those who are reluctant to give their last penny. The recent valuation of the Church property of Negroes at $205,782,612, therefore, requires no comment when they own only about two billion dollars' worth of property altogether.

The average Negro has not been able to rise above the level of the soil. The proclamation of Abraham Lincoln was only the beginning of the solution of the Negro's problem. An overwhelming majority of Negroes live in slums—dwellings which have no running water, lights, proper heating apparatus, improved streets or sewerage. In such locale one finds vice, crime, illegitimacy and prostitution prevalent. With the juvenile court system indifferent and the parents out seeking to make ends meet, children are left to the influence of those environments day in and day out.

[25] W. E. B. DuBois, *The Souls of Black Folk*, Chicago, A. C. McClurg and Co., 1928, pp. 5-6.

BACKGROUNDS OF NEGRO DRAMA

SUMMARY

The first dramatic effort of the American slave was in the form of songs. Those songs were poured forth as a result of two things: (1) the Negro's own innate tendencies, and (2) the bondage of slavery. These canticles served as a sort of inspiration, and gave the idea that somewhere in a glory land there would be rest for the weary, and abundance for the faithful. Similarly, the poetry of the slave was based on his experience as well as his idea of heaven. When one considers the prose that was written between 1790 and 1860, one assumes that it is slightly inferior to the songs and poetry of the same period. This difference was because the Negro was under rigid restrictions, but he could sing when he was not permitted to express himself otherwise. The literary contributions of Negroes from the time of the Civil War to the dawn of the century were eloquently spoken parts of the prolonged drama of freedom. Negro drama since the World War has been influenced by the social and economic forces which have developed since that time.

CHAPTER II

DRAMA IN SPITE OF RESTRICTIONS—MIMICRY

From the very earliest days, the Negro on the stage was forced to the level of mimicry. But the Negro's universal mimicry is neither base, lowly, nor inferior in quality. His very self and all that he says and does may be dramatic. Every angle of his past and present life is deeply dramatized. Even in his sorrow and unfortunate circumstance, the Negro is dramatic. He is capable of smiling broadly through adversity. He can weep, yet at the slightest notice he can discard his present emotion, and address himself to whatever situation is at hand. He has "an eye that tears can on a sudden fill and lips that smile before the tears are gone." No moment ever finds him unprepared. His puns, skits, sketches, and anecdotes are in virtually every home and community in which he resides.[1]

Because the Negro is successful in mimicry, it does not follow that he is not artistic or original. Mimicry within itself is a distinct achievement. Zora Neale Hurston, who has made a study of the subject, says, "The contention that the Negro imitates from a feeling of inferiority is incorrect. He mimics for the love of it . . . He does it as a mocking bird does it, for the love of it, and not because he likes to be like the one imitated.[2]

[1] Zora Neal Hurston, *Mimicry. Negro Anthology*, by Nancy Cunard London, 1934, p. 39.
[2] *Ibid.*, p. 40.

16

DRAMA IN SPITE OF RESTRICTIONS

In the light of observations thus far made, it is needless to wonder that the stage offers the Negro opportunities incomparable to those of any other trade or profession with the exception of medicine and music. That the Negro is equipped for the stage, as a result of a history crammed with continuous drama is a conclusion that is not to be questioned. Similarly, Negro drama has taught the world to realize that the Negro possesses a distinct art which has not been surpassed.[3] It has done more to win the respect, understanding, and appreciation of the majority race than have all of the inter-racial meetings combined.

MINSTRELSY

There is an absence of satisfactory data concerning the rise and development of Negro minstrelsy. As a matter of fact it is hardly possible to discover its genesis. Scattered bits of information in American drama seem not to furnish much authentic information. We do know that it gathered momentum as it progressed, becoming very popular on the large plantations as a form of entertainment for the masters and at the same time making rapid progress on the stage. Charles White, an Ethiopian comedian and manager, asserts that Gottlieb Grampner was the first to adapt the stage to minstrelsy. White bases his assumption on a copy of the Boston *Gazette* of the 30th of December, 1820. On the other hand, some declare that it was Thomas D. Rice who was the first to do minstrel acts. He at least was responsible for the popularity of "Jim Crow." E. S. Conner, who

[3] James Weldon Johnson, *Black Manhattan*, New York, Alfred A. Knopf, 1930, p. 89.

was an actor in the 1820's and 1830's, but a member of the New York *Times* staff of 1881, writes that when he first met Rice in 1826, Rice was doing little Negro bits between the acts at the Columbia Street Theatre. These sketches were based on Rice's study of Negro life in Louisville the summer before. Behind the Louisville Theatre was a stable owned by one Crow. The actors observed that in the stable was employed a Negro slave who was quite dark in complexion, decrepit and deformed, but with a ludicrous limp, and crooned a very interestingly queer tune, the words of which run as follows:[4]

> Wheel about, turn about
> Do jis so
> An everytime I wheel about
> I jump jim crow.

After observing the ludicrous Negro several times, Rice came to realize that if he could impersonate and portray such a character, he would make a "hit" on the stage; whereupon he composed several skits similar to the one he had heard the slave sing. Rice took the numbers to a Louisville audience that called him back twenty times the first night. As a consequence, "jim crow" jumped into fame.

By 1840 minstrelsy was the distinctive form of American amusement. In 1842 Dan Emmett, with four other actors, began what became known as Negro minstrelsy. Thereafter Edwin P. Christy became a star in that sort of amusement. Charles Callender in the '60's and Lew Dockstader, P. T. Barnum, and Primrose and West are well-known names associated with the success of minstrelsy. The companies taking

[4] Maud Cuney Hare, *Negro Musicians and Their Music*, 41-43.

form for this new purpose were the Virginia Minstrels, the Congo Melodists, the Ethiopian Serenaders, and the Georgia Minstrels. With the lone exception of "Disappointed Bride," a light comedy, by J. P. Sampson (1883), nothing of dramatic consequence bearing upon the Negro was done before the advent of Cole, Johnson and Johnson except cork-face comedy.

In the art of creating jazz tunes, jigs, peculiarly fascinating steps and dances, such clowns as Primrose and West of 1893 fame, Lew Johnson, organizer of a plantation minstrel company, and William Kersands, Billy Windom and Wallace King, were unsurpassed. The first successful colored company was the Georgia Minstrels, organized in 1865 by Charles Hicks, a Negro. From then on, Negro minstrel companies came and went in rapid succession. Often these companies found themselves stranded in towns and cities without means of returning home, for the repetitious caricature of lowly Negro life did not please the audience, everywhere. Despite the fact that minstrelsy made a definite place for itself, inadequate rehearsing and a dearth of properties ofttimes reduced the numbers to little less than "wisecracks," shuffling of the feet, lazily nonchalant attitude, and banjo-picking. Nevertheless, the better prepared companies found a livelihood, and were able to thrive. Jank Haverly, for instance, who headed the Callender Minstrels took his company on a tour to California. So successful was the troupe, that in 1881 Haverly took it to Europe where it enjoyed no less a success than it had in America. In 1882, the company returned to America with added zest and strength. Organized under the caption "Callender's Consolidated Spectacular Colored Minstrels," it toured America with marked success. An all-colored minstrel vogue having been established, minstrels were exceptionally popular as well as successful for the remainder of the century, interspersed only by a few musical comedies.

ATTEMPTS AT MORE SERIOUS DRAMA

The year of 1767 marks the beginning of interest in the Negro as dramatic material. In that year was produced the first comic opera in America. "The Disappointment," which was its name, was written by Thomas Forest and produced with an all-white cast. Nevertheless, Raccoon's lines were definitely influenced by Negro dialect, which satirized southern brogue of the time. The following excerpt suggests as much:

RACCOON: Dis is de scheme of Brudder Hum. I second your resolution. Do you gib de challenge, Mr. Buckram?

In 1776, "The Fall of British Tyranny" was written by John Leacock. It is thought that a cast of whites caricatured a group of slaves who agreed that they would turn on their masters upon being set free by the British. In "Yorker's Stratagem," which appeared in 1792, a comic Yankee marries a West Indian mulatto, and thus projects the Negro question upon the American stage.

The entrance of the black thespian on the American stage, however, dates back to 1795 when James Murdock's "The Triumph of Love," or "Reconciliations," was presented with one Sambo playing an important role.[5] Interestingly enough Sambo is not portrayed here as a comic servant. In fact, he plays a romantic role, observing:

[5] Margaret G. Mayorga, *A Short History of the American Drama*, Dodd, Mead and Company, New York: 1932, p. 29.

Dis wool of mine will curl up so Sambo tinks himself
handsome. He very 'complished, too. He sing well, he
dance well; he play fiddle well; can't tink so pretty well.
He berry often tink why he slave to white man.

Though a courageous undertaking, the play has little
that is of social benefit. The lines are crude and
coarsely thrown together, and the dialect is highly
exaggerated.

In 1830 came "A Trip to Niagara," by Dunlap, a
social satire that would challenge the ridicule of Ben
Jonson. As a matter of fact, it concerns itself with
an ironical discussion of the habits and customs of the
age.

Unable to find a white woman to play the role of a
Negro laundress, the producer of "The Tailor in Distress" (1823) used Edwin Forest, who, it is said,
amused the audience delightfully, and was an instant
success. In Anna Cora Mowatt's "Fashion," produced in 1845, Zeke is portrayed as the comic Negro
servant. Various opinions regard "Self" (1856) as
the first skit in which a colored woman appeared.
Who she was or where she was at the time she played
the role of Mammy is not clear.

Negro theatrical talent had been budding for a number of years in restaurants, bar rooms, night clubs, and
gambling houses, where men of the sporting world
came to enjoy the song and drama of the black Bo-
hemians. From such shambles of minstrelsy sprang an
organized group of Negro actors in 1821. Evidence
is to the effect that the group organized themselves in
1821 into the African Company, presented performances of Shakespearean plays, and acquitted themselves with dignity. They also presented other classics
and plays of lighter vein. Charles C. Morean of
New York City has in his possession a bill of the

21

"African Company" at the Theatre in Mercer Street
in the rear of—1 Mile Stone, Broadway. According
to this bill "Tom and Jerry," a comedy, was the show
of the evening. Hutton, basing his opinion on the
observation of Ireland and the New York *National
Advocate* of October 27, 1821, is of the opinion that
this was a company of Negro amateurs who played in
New York in 1820-1821. When that company of
trained amateurs performed in a hotel next door to the
Grove, the *National Advocate* of October 27, 1821,
gave the following notice:

"The gentlemen of color announce another play at their
Pantheon, corner of Bleecher and Mercer Streets, on
Monday Evening."

According to the Annals of the Stage by George C.
D. Odell, one Brown directed the production. The
actors were Williams as Tom, Jackson as Jerry, Bates
as Bob, Miss Davis as Kate, and Miss Foot as Sue.
The prices of admission to the African show were high
for current purses: boxes, seventy-five cents; pit, fifty
cents, and gallery, thirty-seven and a half cents. Professor Odell further recalls that a bill states.[6]

"On June 20, 21, 1823 at the Theatre in Mercer Street,
in the rear of — 1 Mile Stone, Broadway, the performers
of the African Company have kindly consented to give their
services in order to contribute a 'Benefit' to their manager,
Mr. Brown, who for the first time throws himself. on the
liberality of a generous public."

The performance of the occasion was the drama of
"King Shotaway," founded on facts taken from the
insurrection of the Island of St. Vincent, written from
experiences of Brown.[7] James Hewlett who sub-

[6] G. C. D. O'Dell, *Annals of the New York Stage*, p. 70.
[7] *Ibid.*, p. 70.

DRAMA IN SPITE OF RESTRICTIONS

sequently organized a Negro company which interpreted classical scripts, played King Shotaway.

ANTI-SLAVERY DRAMA

Drama in spite of itself is always propaganda, and
the abolitionists early used the stage to attack slavery.
The "Star of Emancipation," by the Massachusetts
Female Society, of 1841 had a decided effect upon the
institution of slavery. As borne out by its preface,
"Star of Emancipation" appeared before the public
with no great pretensions. One reads in that preface,
"We do not vie with Virgil or Shakespeare in point
of plot or tragedy." The play, as its authors admit is
not a drama of first magnitude. The lines which were
written by various individuals run as follows:[8]

Persevere in the spirit of energetic,
And believing prayer, and you must conquer
At last, your cause is that of justice
Humanity, benevolence, and religion.
Go on then with courage, and fearlessness
The God of love is with you!
He will not suffer your effort to prove abortive.

The "Star of Emancipation" is simply the story of
the trials and tribulations of slaves, honestly told,
describing in a penchant, terse style the efforts of
slaves in trying to escape, and their hardships and
undernourishment on their mapless journey. The
piece describes how many of the slaves who attempted
to escape were captured, bound, brutishly beaten, and
cast with bleeding wounds into the walls of an old
prison house.

Carlos, a field slave, was depicted as a composite of

[8] *Star of Emancipation*, Boston, Massachusetts, Female Society, 1841, p. 25.

thousands of his peers. And though he suffered, he was brave, determined, daring, always willing to risk his life, to do anything to get away from his unbearable bondage, and finding supreme happiness only when he reached free soil, "the blessed aid of Liberty so sweet." There is no question but that the play made tremendous appeal to America on behalf of slaves.

In melodramatic fashion "The Branded Hand," which appeared in 1845, depicted the evils of slavery. It did not reach a large audience, however, and no one knows exactly how much it influenced public opinion. In 1852 "Uncle Tom's Cabin," the Harriet Beecher Stowe piece, which has toured the world, playing over and over since the Civil War, was dramatized. It is the story dealing with the tribulations and vicissitudes of Uncle Tom and the death of little Eva.

The hardships of Uncle Tom began with his auction by one Shelby, the owner, who found himself in dire financial straits. "I'm sorry," he said to his wife, Emily, "I'm sorry this thing takes hold of you so. The fact is, Emily, the thing is done, the bills of sale are already signed"; and Uncle Tom is sold and resold until he falls into the evil and vicious hands of Legree whom Miss Stowe sets up as a type of thousands of slave holders of the deep South.

This observation will indicate the material of which he is made: "Tom, I mean to promote ye, and make a driver of ye. Now take this here gal and flog her. Ye've seen enough on't to know how." When he refuses, Tom's troubles multiply. During the torture of one of his innumerable beatings, it appears to him that even the Lord has forgot him. So, at least, is the indication of this expression, "O, Jesus! Lord Jesus, have you forgot us poor creatures. Help, Lord, I perish." This dramatic piece comes to a melodramatic ending with the death of its hero who refuses "to squeal" on a fellow slave.[9]

Though southern folk have attempted to ignore this stirring drama with its flashbacks to their doorsteps, its theme moving quickly from violation of enslaved women to pitiless cruelty of shackled men, "Uncle Tom's Cabin" has been performed before more people than any known Negro production with the possible exception of "Green Pastures,"[10] which is considered by Burns Mantle as the drama of the age. There seems to be no estimate of how many millions of people throughout the world have wept over the tribulations of Uncle Tom. Just how much weight it had in precipitating the Civil War also remains a question.

In *Dred*, which Mrs. Stowe later produced, she did not show much change except to soften her attitudes, for she still painted the Negro as the meek and submissive being who should be treated humanely, and the mulatto as a superior entitled to the rights of whites.[11]

"Experience," or, "How to Give a Northern Man a Backbone" (1856), by William Wells Brown, a Negro, catalogues the experiences of a supposedly fractious slave. So numerous were the demands that Brown give readings from this play that he was compelled to forego much of his regular work so that he could devote his time to the delivery of his lyceum lectures, and the reading of his play.[12]

[9] Julia Cline, "Rise of the American Stage Negro," *Drama Magazine*, January, 1931, pp. 9-10, 14.
[10] James W. Johnson, *Contributions of the Negro*, unpublished.
[11] H. B. Stowe, *Deed*, Boston, 1856.
[12] *Liberator*, August 1, 1856, XVI, p. 124.

THE NEGRO AND THE DRAMA

The scene of action moves from Boston to the South into which a pastor is sold as a slave. Immediately upon his arrival, he falls upon evil days, in that he is subjected to the "breaking in process," a severe torture experienced by slaves, who had ever been free. He remains in the South long enough to be "convinced" that his impressions of the South had been taken from the wrong point of view. The piece comes to a thrilling climax with the escape of a fugitive slave to Canada.

Despite defective technique the play has intrinsic merit, with many graphic and commendable lines. It is observed that as Brown interpreted the passages that caused the slave to tremble and to burst forth into an eloquent plea for freedom, tears trickled from the eyes of nearly every one present.

Brown added to his "Experience," another piece. The scene of this play, "Life at the South," is laid in the land of slaves, and it deals with the social injustice of bondage. It is a play embracing the elements of truth, style, courage, theme and heroism.[13] Of Brown and his play the Poughkeepsie *Daily Eagle* observed:

"William Wells Brown is a competent witness to the evils of slavery, having been for many years under the lash, and he has redeemed himself therefrom to speak in eloquent and effective words against the sum of all villainies. His lectures are among the best ever delivered on that subject, as all who heard him testify, and his drama interested and amused his audience, bringing the subject before them more vividly than any amount of argument could have done. It seemed to have been highly relished by the audience."

[13] *Liberator*, April 4, 1862, p. 54.

DRAMA IN SPITE OF RESTRICTIONS

"The Escape" (1858), also by William Wells Brown, is not so pretentious; yet it does possess light and sharp satire on the institution of slavery.

Attempting to satirize the fugitive slave law, J. T. Trowbridge wrote in 1857 "Neighbor Jackwood." Based on an ideal situation rather than an actual one, the heroine escapes from her locale in the South to New England. She is tracked down and captured, only to be rescued by a white hero, who marries her. Taking hold of the creole vogue, Mrs. Mary Putnam produced two light skinned girls in her "Tragedy of Errors" (1862), patterned after Shakespeare's "Comedy of Errors." In this story, however, the characters are not aware of their identity until it is revealed they had at one time been Negro slaves.

"Ossawatomie Brown" (1859), by J. C. Swayze, concerns itself with the Harper's Ferry raid in which John Brown, the abolitionist, attempted to set the Negro free. The point of the play was to show the role the Negro played in the insurrection.

A Negro theme was ably treated by Dion Boucicault in his dramatized version of "The Octoroon" (1859). Moreover, "The Octoroon" was a distinct improvement over anything hither produced concerning the Negro. Aside from its propaganda and ridicule, it is charged with melodramatic interest.

With the possible exception of "Uncle Tom's Cabin," "The Octoroon" is the best play dealing with the Negro presented prior to the Civil War. It possesses all of the attributes of a real drama: theme, plot, style, heroism, and dènouement. Interesting, too, is the fact that the piece is not soaked with dialect, even though it sprang from the depth of slavery.

The lines spoken by Zoe, the Octoroon, in a scene

27

with George Peyton illustrate the general tone of the play:

ZOE: (aside) Alas! he does not know, he does not know, and will despise me, when he learns who, what he has so loved (aloud). Pleading for the hand of Dora, he says to George, "O forgive me! Yes, I love you—I did not know it until your words showed me what has been in my heart. . . . . . and now I know how unhappy I am. (*Here he is cognizant of the fact that he can never marry the girl he loves, because he was cursed by Cain. Bemoaning the fact that one-eighth of his blood is black, he realizes that quantity poisons all the rest, however bright, red, the other may be.*)

A powerful drama, well written, and often well acted, "The Octoroon" has had a cherished history on the stage. Produced first by Joseph Jefferson at the Olympic Theatre, September 3, 1866, in New York City, the play has been presented up and down the country ever since.[14]

This play was satirized by W. H. Peck with his *Moctroon*. An answer came also in "Colonel Carter of Cartersville," by Angus Thomas, in Mark Twain's "Pudd'nhead Wilson," and Steele Mackaye's "A Fool's Errand," which retained the idea of the comic Negro as dominant.

THE NEGRO ACTOR PRIOR TO THE TWENTIETH CENTURY TRAGEDY

The pursuit of drama for the sake of art itself, however, was not foreign to the Negro even before the Civil War. The realization that the role Othello, of Shakespeare's "The Moor of Venice," could be acted by Negroes led Frederick Ira Aldridge to become in-

[14] Thomas Hamilton, *The Anglo-African Magazine*. New York: Vol. I, 1859, pp. 63-64.

terested in the interpretation of the lines of the central character.[15]

FREDERICK IRA ALDRIDGE

Aldridge's stage interest began early, for we find him in the character of Rola, the hero in Sheridan's "Pizarro," with a Negro cast in a New York Theatre, as a boy in his teens. He also played and sang leading roles in opera. Charles Matthews writes, "He played the role of Baillie MacWhapple in a Romantic grand opera; he also sang in 'Opposum up a Gum Tree.' "[16] Then he became a stage hand at the Chatham Theatre where he enjoyed the opportunity of listening to the interpretation of lines. At the suggestion of his con-

[15] About the middle of the nineteenth century the family antecedent of Ira Aldridge seems to be shrouded in obscurity. Such, however, was the misfortune of many Negroes born in America before the Civil War. There is some evidence to the effect that his grandfather was brought to the United States as a slave, and that he was sold to a Maryland plantation owner. Ira's father, Daniel Aldridge, was apparently born in Maryland. There is still another interesting story about the tragedian's birth and growth—that his grandfather was an African chief, and that he was brought to this country by missionaries to be educated; that Daniel was born, educated, and married in this country without experiencing slavery. Be that as it may, his father was at one time a resident of New York City, where two sons were probably born. Ira and his brother attended the New York African School. With him as fellow students one discovers Dr. James McCune Smith and Alexander Crummel. In an article written by Dr. Smith from Ireland where he had just seen Ira Aldridge in "Othello," the statement that he was not a bright pupil is made. Factual data regarding his birth and youth have been difficult to obtain. Most of the scholars until only recently, relied on the sketches of Simmons in his "Men of Mark," and the writings of William Wells Brown. These men gave as his birthplace Bell-Air, Maryland. However, in the petition and affidavit of Ira Aldridge himself in obtaining naturalization as a British subject, he wrote that he was born in New York on June 24, 1807.—Hamilton, *op. cit.*, 63-64.

[16] Charles Matthews, *Sketches of Celebrated Trip to America,* 1824, p. 9.

temporaries—Patrick Reason, Samuel Ringgold Ward and Alexander Crummell, who subsequently became engraver, orator and preacher respectively, Aldridge gave up the job as stage assistant to return to the African Free School. He was soon sent to Glasgow where he studied for a year and a half, making a splendid scholarship record, with several prizes and a medal in Latin. Still school had no charm for Ira as compared with the theatre. So we trail him from Glasgow to London where after considerable work and effort, he was allowed to make his first appearance as Othello in 1826. His performance was an instant success. He met with even greater acclaim in the provinces. Subsequently, he played in repertoire in most of the capitals of Europe. Aldridge's performance in English with a German company, the first venture of its kind, that is, a black hero and white heroine on the stage, was awaited with anxious trepidation; but his impersonation proved so convincing that his appearance turned out to be most successful, as well as a personal triumph for himself and company. The King of Prussia conferred the title of Chevalier upon him. He was knighted by the King of Sweden and decorated by the Emperor of Russia. He married a Swedish baroness by whom he had three children.

Meanwhile, Ira played other leading roles.[17] In his interpretation of "King Lear," he wore a flesh colored skull from which hung grey curly locks—covering his kinky hair. A piece of wax gave an arch to his flat nose. It is said that he played the role of the aged king, who was persecuted by his wicked daughters, better than he played the Moor of Venice. It is agreed by those who saw him act that he was superb in his in-

[17] Hamilton, *op. cit.*, pp. 63-64.

dignation and anger, mingled with feebleness and tremblings, portraying every attribute and characteristic of the wretched old king. The marvelous acting and success of the ebony actor, stirred the emulation of Somoliloff, the great Russian comedian, to play in the Alexander Theatre, "Othello" and "King Lear" with a truly Shakespearean vivacity of imagination.

Aldridge starred also in two plays of later production. Three quarters of a century after "Othello" another drama dealing with Negro theme and character was written. This was the story of "Oroonoko," by Thomas Southerne. The hero is an African Prince, stolen from his native Kingdom of Angola during the reign of Charles the Second, and sold into slavery in one of the British possessions. The heroine, a charmingly beautiful maiden, daughter of the Lieutenant Governor of the Islands, fell in love with him at first sight. Although the piece is highly dramatic, respected and well written, it has not been played for many years on either the English or the American stage. During the course of his dramatic climb and even after he reached the pinnacle, Aldridge gave various performances of "Oroonoko," at the Coburg and elsewhere.

"Mungo," the other play, a comic opera, was written by Isaac Bickerstaffe in 1768,[18] the year in which it was presented at Drury Lane. The story centers around a slave owned by one Don Diego, a West Indian Planter. Typical of the theme of the opera is a song sung by Mungo:[19]

[18] Isaac Bickerstaff, *The Padlock, A Comic Opera.*
[19] *Ibid.,* p. 24.

Dear heart what a terrible life
A dog has a better sheltered and fed
Night and day, 'tis de fame.
We wish to de Lord we was dead.
Whatever to be done,
Poor black must run
Mongo here, Mongo dere,
Mongo everywhere.

That Aldridge played the lead in "Mongo" the critics do not doubt.[20] Laurence Hutton is of the opinion that Aldridge occasionally played Mongo in his natural form. Just when his portrayal of Mongo took place there is no authentic record. Data pieced together would lead one to suppose that his interpretation of the role came before he decided to leave London to explore Continental Europe and the provinces. However, it might have been after his successful run at Covent Garden where he played "Othello," April 10, 1833; at least for a long time he was unable to get work commensurate with his training and ability.

He had known success and approbation as few Negroes of his age had. Likewise he had known humiliation, sacrifice, disappointment and abuse. And he had surmounted what others had considered obstacles.[21] Having won fame, he was now ready to return to America where he had made his beginning, to fill an engagement in New York City. Failing health compelled him to cancel his trip. His task ended, he died August 7, 1867, at Lodes, Poland.

VICTOR SÉJOUR

Second only to Ira Aldridge, if not superior in the

[20] Laurence Hutton, The American Stage Negro, *Curiosities of the Stage.* New York: Harper and Brothers, 1891, p. 96.
[21] M. Smith, The Negro as an Artist, *The Radical*, Vol. II, 1867, pp. 40-42.

field of drama was Victor Séjour. He was born in New Orleans, June 2, 1817, the illegitimate child of Juan Francisco and Louis Victor Séjour, according to Tinker.[22] Larousse says he was born in Paris in 1821. Recognition came to him when he wrote poems on the anniversary of the Société d'Economie des Artisans, an organization of which he was a member. In 1836 his parents, who were now married, sent him to Paris to complete his studies and to be away from the embarrassment suffered by other colored children. In Paris he received literary notice upon the composition of a poem entitled "Le Retour de Napoleon" (1841). This poem had much to do with his entering the literary circle of Paris, meeting such luminaries as Alexander Dumas and Emile Augier.

His friendship with Augier influenced his interest in drama. Le Thêâtre-Francais, in 1844, presented his first play, "Diegarias." In 1849, his "La Chute de Sejan," which bears a resemblance to Ben Jonson's play of the same name, was produced. The theatres of Paris presented twenty-one of his plays, two of which were worked out in collaboration with Theodore Barrière, one with Bresil and one with Jaimi. His plays were so enjoyable that all of the drama lovers of Paris turned out the first night to see them. Until the moment of curtain time Séjour would make revisions in his plays, giving the actors slips of paper on which were written his corrections. During the last intermission or after the first four acts of "Fils de la Nuit," he successfully altered the fifth act.[23] His understanding of audience psychology and reaction

[22] Larocque Tinker, *Les Poètes de Langue Française*, Paris, Librairie Ancienne Honoré Champion, 1932, pp. 427-428.
[23] Tinker, *op. cit.*, p. 429.

was remarkable. He studied the audience equally as much as he did the drama.

Meanwhile, the element of time had had its effect and public taste no longer relished Sèjour's brand of play. He trudged from producer to producer with "Cromwell" and "The Vampire," two fantastic comedies, before the Gaiety Theatre finally agreed to produce "The Vampire." By this time Séjour was nearly exhausted with tuberculosis, dying September 20, 1874.

Observing exhibitions of such talent in Negroes, Morgan Smith wrote thus in 1867 of the "Negro As Artist," in Volume II of *The Radical*, "Many years of familiar knowledge of the Negro has convinced me that Negroes are born artists, orators, painters, sculptors, musicians and actors—though dwarfed by the wicked magician, oppression." Smith had seen exhibitions of one James, a slave. He said further, "If 30,000,000 Americans were not mostly fools, they would seize upon the great opportunity of today . . . obtain from the Negro race that tropical glow, that imagination and passion. But equally will the Negro when his opportunity shall come, as it must, shine in the dramatic art."

SUMMARY

The Negro's first contribution to drama was mimicry, which merely interested casual observers. Out of this developed minstrelsy which found its way to the stage. Next the Negro became a comic character on the stage as seen by white playwrights and actors. Then came the abolition drama which was intended to aid emancipation. In legitimate drama, however, Ira Aldridge as an actor, and Victor Séjour as a playwright, gave the world a new conception of the Negro on the stage.

34

CHAPTER III

Drama With Less Restriction

It required much time for the American theater-goers to look at a play based altogether on the Negro life even if it were caricature. They could more easily endure Negro songs interspersed here and there in other plays, and the Negro song was often a short one-act play. It dramatized the life of the Negro, and did it so successfully that an unwilling public had to give attention.

For a short time after the Civil War the old plantation songs held sway on the American stage, but in freedom the Negro himself and those who observed his reaction to the new order portrayed him in a new type of song in contradistinction to the songs of slavery days. The slave songs were such as "Old Folks at Home," "Old Black Joe," "Old Uncle Ned," and "Massa's in de Cold, Cold Ground."

In the change from the plantation etiquette to that of the independent freedom, the Negro lost the obsequiousness expressed in "Marse John" and "Miss Lucy" and became conscious of the joy of living as Mister Jim himself. The Negro still had a sense of humor, however, and saw in himself something at which he could laugh. Whites thus observant caricatured the Negro in his new role as a bunglesome imitator, trying to take over suddenly modern culture on the periphery of which he had been formerly compelled to remain. Here then the Negro was no longer

35

the docile "darky"; he was the ridiculous "coon."
The contempt for this new Negro was expressed in the
song, "Go 'way Back and Sit Down." The "darky
songs" remained among those sentimentally attached
to slavery. They were often sung in the homes and
sometimes on the stage as encores, but the new generation of both races understood better and enjoyed
the "coon songs." With the noble exception of
"Carry Me Back to Old Virginny," written in 1878
by James Bland, a Negro himself, that post-bellum
period produced no additional "darky songs" of consequence. To these Bland added others of less merit,
"Oh Dem Golden Slippers" (1879), "De Golden Wedding" (1880), "In the Morning by the Bright Light"
(1880), and "In the Evening by the Moonlight"
(1880).

The Negro's interpretation of the meaning of his
new freedom was caricatured in

> Good by, hard work widout no pay
> I's gwine up North, whar good folks say
> Dat white wheat-bread and a dollar a day
> Is a comin', comin'.

In the "coon songs" the Negro joy shone forth in such
as "Whistling Rufus" and "Smoky Mokes," which
gave new life to the old-fashioned cake-walk about the
end of the last century. Likewise in "Gib me, oh,
gib me, oh, how I wish you would, dat watermillion
hangin' on de vine." Ragtime and syncopation were
swaying the entire country.

In the rapid rise of some members of the race came
the exultation from the thought that the problem of
the freedom had been solved and the Negro could
triumphantly express his joy on seeing the bottom rail

becoming the top one, and he sang "I've Got a White Man Working for Me." Disappointment and disillusionment came, however, in such songs as "Rufus Rastus Johnson Brown, what are you going to do when the rent comes 'round"; and still further in the song "When you ain't got no money, well, you needn't come 'round; if you is broke Mister Nigger I'll throw you down."* Later S. H. Dudley had this thought of economic difficulty in singing, "Come after breakfast, bring your lunch with you, but leave before dinner time."

Negro personal relationships which found little portrayal before the Civil War except here and there in the lamentations of the abolition drama were nevertheless dramatized almost in detail in the caricaturing "coon songs." In one of these a Negro sang to his girl:

> Good-bye, Eliza Jane, I'm gwine a' for to leave you,
> Well, you'll know, when I go, that I was the fellow
> With the dough.

To this his girl was made to reply

> Don't you hear your lady love a softly calling, Alexander,
> Take me to your heart again and call me honey,
> All I want is loving, I don't want your money,
> Alexander, tell me, don't you love your baby no more?

The story is advanced further in such family discord as is expressed in "Ain't dat a shame, a measly shame, to keep your honey out in de rain?" This tone deepens into the touching appeal in "Won't you open dat door and let me in? I stand yer freezin', wet to do skin." The penitent woman, however, shows just as much concern for her lover in

*Quoted with permission from Henry Von Tilzer Music Publishing Company, New York City.

37

THE NEGRO AND THE DRAMA

Won't you come home, Bill Bailey, won't you come home?
I'll do the cooking, darling, I'll pay de rent,
I knows I've done you wrong.
'Member dat rainy eve dat I drove you out,
Wid nothing but a fine tooth comb?
I know I'se to blame, well, ain't dat a shame?
Bill Bailey, won't you please come home?[1]

The Negro in this high glee of life often advanced
too far and was caught in the toils of the law and
had to say, "Please, Mr. Johnson, turn me loose, I got
no money but a good excuse." When pleading that
he was just there and was not the culprit, the police-
man, as Ernest Hogan pictured the situation, sang
"All Coons Look Alike to Me." Friends cautioned
the pleasure seeking freedmen not to live so fast and
to hold on to the religious precepts of the fathers of
the race. The high-flyer often tried to reform when
brought face to face with the horrors of hell, but just
as often he backslid because of the joy he found in
fast life. He had some consolation, however, in singing:

I'm goin' live anyhow until I die,
I know this kind of living ain't very high;
With sticks and stones
You may break my bones
Talk about me all you want
When I'm dead and gone
I'm goin' to live anyhow until I die.

What had these songs to do with legitimate drama?
Everything. They were a dramatization of the Negro in freedom. There was much exaggeration, to be
sure, but the portraiture had some foundation in fact.
With the cakewalk, a little dialogue, the dance, and

[1] The last two songs are quoted by permission of Paul Pio-
neer Music Corporation, New York.

the "Pas-mah-la" these songs made up the musical comedies which so highly entertained theater-goers throughout the United States with ragtime and syncopation. These shows had such long runs in New York City that they indicated the coming of a black Broadway.

The Negro was to have a new day in drama. Ambitious playwrights of the race had long been anxious to bring a higher degree of artistry to Negro songs, with an idea of displacing the "coon songs" which had as their themes jamborees, razors "with the gastronomical delights of chicken, pork chops and watermelons, and the experiences of their red-hot 'mamas' and their never too faithful 'papas.' "[2]

The Negro's really dynamic influence was felt in Broadway theatrical circles at about the turn of the century. "Clorindy," written by Paul Laurence Dunbar, and Will Marion Cook, had been a success. "Jes Lak White Folks" had, by no means, been a failure. Not being able to persuade Dunbar to collaborate with him on a full-length opera to be called "The Cannibal King," Cook turned the matter over to James Weldon Johnson who, within a short while, had the piece nearly completed when differences of opinion developed between the two, and the unfinished work was sold for three hundred dollars.

This disagreement, however, did not daunt Johnson's spirits. On the contrary, it enhanced them; for his brother, and Bob Cole, with reasonable dispatch, did the featured songs for the "Bell of Bridgeport," written for May Irwin. On the completion of the assignment, the trio wrote music for Peter Daily's play,

[2] James Weldon Johnson, *Along This Way*, p. 149.

"Champagne Charlie," which was followed by their writing a two-act comedy, "The Supper Club," produced by the Sire brothers at the Winter Garden.[3] The outstanding stars of the period acted in "The Supper Club." Among them were Virginia Earle, Ada Lewis, Toby Claude, Alexander Clark, Thomas Q. Seabrook, and Jennie McCree.

The production numbers that blazoned the names of Cole, Johnson, and Johnson across New York headlines were the songs they wrote for "The Sleeping Beauty." For this production, they wrote three numbers: "Tell Me, Dusky Maiden," "Come Out, Dinah, on the Green," and "Nobody's Looking but the Owl and the Moon." Upon the presentation of this comedy, they at once appeared in the headlines of the newspapers as the ranking writers of Broadway musical shows. The song that sent them to the top rung of the theatre during the 1901-02 season, and at the same time brought to them a handsome check, was "The Maiden with the Dreamy Eyes," sung by Anna Held in "The Little Duchess." The song was a great favorite, not only on the stage, but among young men calling to see their sweethearts. The lyric was to be sung by the beaux as they gave musical expression to their feelings and sentiments.[4] The first stanza is:

> There are eyes of blue,
> There are brown eyes too,
> There are eyes of every size,
> And eyes of every hue;
> But I surmise
> That if you are wise
> You'll be careful of the maiden
> With the dreamy eyes.

[3] James Weldon Johnson, *op. cit.*, p. 165.
[4] *Ibid.*, 175.

DRAMA WITH LESS RESTRICTION

By the time "The Maiden with the Dreamy Eyes" had become well known, "Under the Bamboo Tree"[5] written by Bob Cole followed, and the financial worries of the three brown, Broadway personalities were momentarily at an end. Success and prosperity were theirs. Bob Cole, Johnson and Johnson then were engaged to write exculsively for Klaw and Erlanger Productions, the largest company of its kind in the country at the time. Forthwith, they also became members of the producing staff.

During the early spring of 1905, the trio started for the second time over the Orpheum Circuit, the trip taking them as far west as California. On returning to New York, the trio found that they had a six-week engagement in London, where they later played with satisfaction and dignity. The two hundred songs which they had written by 1906 had made them internationally famous.

BURLESQUE

Beginning casually in 1908, and continuing from 1910 until the Great War, Negro musical comedy which had been on Broadway, now took up its residence in Harlem, at the Lafayette Theatre at 132nd Street and 7th Avenue. The South since Reconstruction days had had its separate houses for entertainment. S. H. Dudley since 1910 had been establishing small burlesque houses in the District of Columbia and vicinity. Negroes had not yet migrated to Boston in large numbers, and those that were there shared seating space with the whites. Chicago had relegated Negroes to the South side where they built the Pekin

[5] Bob Cole, *Under the Bamboo Tree*, J. W. Sterne, 1902.

41

Theatre. Washington had built the Howard Theatre where stock companies went for a week's engagement. Much later John T. Gibson built the Standard Theatre in Baltimore. For the most part, except in the larger eastern cities, Negroes who attended burlesque shows had been perched back in the galleries, commonly referred to as "peanut gallery." On the contrary, with the coming of these elaborate buildings, Negroes had something of which to feel proud.

The Lafayette Theatre went a step farther than the other new theatres, in that it organized its own players. And again it was verified that the Negro could not only do light comedy, but also serious drama. The Lafayette Players did artistically and efficiently such pieces as "The Servant in the House," "The Love of Choo Chin" and "Madam X."[6] Polite society, however, was not long to enjoy this class of entertainment. The bulk of the black population still preferred black-face comedy, with a copious supply of hilarity under a corked face. Actors and producers began to realize that the Negro audience as a whole had not developed a lofty attitude toward the art of drama. And accordingly, as Negroes playing to Negro audiences, with no restrictions or reprimands forthcoming, actors easily threw off all inhibitions, and gave their audiences the type of burlesque and low-brow comedy that made them merry to their own satisfaction. Despite a wealth of talent, including such names as Sidney Kirkpatrick, Walker Thompson, Clarence Muse, Irvin C. Miller, and others of merit, the best Negro production between 1910 and 1917 was "Dark Town Follies." When it opened at the Lafayette Theatre in October, 1913, aside from playing to

[6] James Weldon Johnson, *Black Manhattan*, pp. 102-105.

Negroes, it brought, as a result of favorable newspaper space given it, theatre-goers from other sections
of New York. It was a type of comedy which New
Yorkers again desired. Its soothing syncopation,
quaint songs, and new dance hits were well executed.
It is said that Florenz Ziegfeld was so greatly impressed with the show that he borrowed the little song,
"Rock Me in the Cradle of Love," a song that dis-
proved the assumption that Negroes could not do romantic scenes and numbers.[7]

Negroes Playing to Negro Audiences

Except in rare instances when Negro actors were
playing exclusively to Negro audiences, critics fairly
agreed that when the curtain rose on a Negro scene, it
was nothing more than burlesque farce and hilarious
comedy. One character, for instance, would be dressed
in shoes, suit, and hat that would come more nearly
fitting a man three times his size; whereas, another
character would wear an outfit very much too small
for his build.

The most popular selections of these comedians
were the Blues, which are solos dealing with the first
person. The aim of these Blues is to describe the
soloist's hardships, love affairs, cruel treatment, prison
confinement, and reaction toward a judge when sentenced. In brief, the theme of the Blues widely varies.
W. C. Handy, recognized as the father of Blues, published, in 1918, a Blues anthology which furnished the
Negro a number of funny solos. These new versions
of hardships usually brought forth laughter.

Another device which has been used to kindle the

[7] James Weldon Johnson, *op. cit.*, p. 175.

flame of laughter has been to construct a short piece that has dealt with the folk of the immediate community, often the point being to make a joke at the expense of a well known local person. Then there would be a girl of the jazz-singing variety, ludicrous in song as well as inharmonious in dress, whose husky voice set her off as one of the featured attractions. She was supported usually by a chorus of brown skin models, dressed with extreme brevity. Another feature popular with the audience was the discovery by a couple of husbands that their wives had been playing truant, or in the vernacular of the comedians, had been "stepping out with another man." On making this discovery, the husbands would display their knives, guns, and razors, explaining how they would prepare the delinquent transgressors for the undertakers. Moreover, there were other such skits as: "I'll knock you from a mazing grace to a floatin' apple dumple." "I don't see you at all, just see something floatin' around where your mouth ought to be," and "You are too ugly to die natural, you are just going to ugly yourself away." Such buffoonery, in addition to a moving picture reel, concluded a three-hour program.

INDEPENDENT EFFORT

Leigh Whipper, who was trained for law at Howard University, finding his profession none too lucrative, came to New York at the turn of the century to try for short stage skits. In his possession is a rare scrapbook of news clippings that traces the developments of the colored thespian from then on. From this scrapbook we glean that as early as 1890 one Sam Jack of burlesque reputation became convinced of the idea that the Negro could not only do minstrel acts and stunts,

44

but also could do other types that would reflect credit upon himself and his race. Embracing this opinion, he organized a company of singers, and dancers, consisting of four men and sixteen damsels, making its debut as "The Creole Show of New York." The excellent dancing of the troupe, the beautifully designed costumes, and the snappy songs, differing considerably from the old plantation minstrels, made it at once the theatrical talk of New York. With an interchange of short speeches, in the form of dialogues, monologues, and soliloquies, the show was indeed outstanding among Negro entertainments.

Sensing that there was a wealth of financial and ecstatic compensation in this sort of newly discovered smart entertainment, a host of similar producers and independent actors sprang up. Among the first were Williams and Walker and Cole and Johnson with their cleverly constructed comedies, consistently and persistently rehearsed until the casts were quite capable of embarking on tours, which took them to the eastern and western sections of the United States and abroad.[8] The career of Jesse A. Ship, a man of theatrical genius, was an important factor in these developments.

These all-Negro companies traveled as far east as Boston, where they played to packed houses of appreciative audiences, as far west as California, stopping over in Chicago, where they were the delight of the World's Fair of 1893, and to London where they played in fashionable circles. Upon their return to New York they were graciously received, and played to sensational houses. The Creole Show continued in successful tour for three seasons before disbanding.

[8] James Weldon Johnson, *op cit.*, pp. 102-105.

From its remains and with the addition of other talent, another show, "The Octoroon," was organized. The performances of the latter consisted of an intermixture of songs, dances, and minstrelsy, supervised by John W. Isham who had a gift in producing the kind of comedy that was to the liking of gay New Yorkers. In this satirical and humorous farce, Isham introduced the famous cake-walk dance, which reached its height by the dawn of the century.

To crown his success, Isham followed "The Octoroon" with the production of "Oriental America," a somewhat classical type of presentation, omitting plantation melodies and burlesque entirely. In addition to a charming chorus of girls, he brought together the best musical talent of the country. Boston, then the seat of classical music, furnished him with Sidney Woodward, a trained tenor. Rosamond Johnson, Maggie Scott and others of conservatory training were in his cast. Their artistic interpretation of selections from Faust, Rigoletto, and Carmen, caused Broadway to embrace "Oriental America" with receptive arms.[9]

Bob Cole, already mentioned herein, was no less known in theatrical circles than John Isham. Cole was to light comedy at the turn of the century what Irvin C. Miller was to it a quarter of a century later. Cole's specialty was writing shows. He became known for his subtly written scripts. Aside from the ability to write song and dance comedy, he knew the theatre inside and out. He could design costumes, construct properties, direct a cast, prompt the interpretation of lines, dance, act, and sing. In 1893, he was engaged by a theatrical producer of New York City to write for their all-Negro show featuring Sis-

[9] J. W. Johnson, *Black Manhattan*, 207.

sieretta Jones of "Black Patti" fame, a woman of
musical ability, who displayed her talent at Madison
Square Garden and at the White House before President Harrison. With such facility did Cole compose
the songs for "Black Patti" that, together with her
own innate ability, she won the hearty acclaim of
white southern audiences, a fact not before attained
by dramatic persons of color.

Because of serious differences with the sponsors of
the Troubadours in which "Black Patti" was the
featured attraction, Bob Cole came to the conclusion
that his talent was being exploited, and wrote for himself independently. His venture resulted in producing
"A Trip to Coontown" in 1898. This was among the
first all-Negro productions that came within the realm
of Aristotle's definition of drama, — that is, possessing serious action, with a beginning, a middle, and an
ending, and embracing continuity, plot and theme.[10]
Moreover, it was the second all-Negro show that
definitely received Broadway notice. Negro vaudeville of minor character immediately followed, perhaps
the most noteworthy, "Jes Lak White Folks," a play-
let which should be remembered, if for no other reason
than that it gave Abbie Mitchell her start to fame.

In the meantime, the team of Williams and Walker
were making a vaudeville reputation for itself, tour-
ing the country doing short skits and singing catchy
songs of their own composition. On arriving in New
York in 1896, their appearance having been anxiously
awaited, they were immediately presented in the
"Gold Bug" at the Casino Theatre. For sundry
reasons, the production was not to the liking of sophisticated theatre-goers. Nevertheless, the ambi-

· [10] *The Portico*, Butcher's Translation, Chapter VI.

tious Williams and Walker were by no means dis-
couraged, for they forthwith received a nine-month
contract, under the direction of Koster and Bial, to
introduce to fashionable society the popular cakewalk.
This feat completed the break with the minstrel tradition, notwithstanding the innumerable vicissitudes,
struggles, and ups-and-downs during the interim.
By 1902, the team ranked among the best in the field
of their specialty.[11] In the fall of that year, "In Dahomey" opened at the Fifty-Sixth Street Theatre, in
the heart of New York's theatrical center. Their run
of several weeks[12] in "In Dahomey" enabled the team
to regain fully its bearing; whereupon they organized
a stronger combination, including the Cole and Johnson aggregation, and S. H. Dudley. Dudley also
toured the country independently with his "Smart
Set." Despite the fact that caricature was still the
strongest feature of the Negro actor, he nevertheless,
was acting out a well constructed plot, accompanied
by excellent dancing and music.

There are still to be found many theatre-goers who
readily recall the hilarity and mirth they experienced
at the advent of the century when such shows as "Bandana Land," "Rufus and Rastus," "Abyssinia," and
"Mr. Lode of Kole" furnished much of the glee and
joyousness of Times Square night life. Prolonged
and strenuous work in "Bandana Land" was so tax-
ing that the health of Walker became completely un-
dermined, causing him and his co-worker to be displaced in fame and prominence by the inimitable Bert
Williams, whose reputation on the theatrical scene was
fully established by 1910.

[11] Montgomery Gregory, "The Drama of Negro Life," in
The New Negro, p. 153.
[12] "The Negro on the Stage," *Theatre Magazine*, April,
1903, p. 95.

DRAMA WITH LESS RESTRICTION

That Bert Williams was the idol of the histrionic public, critics have had not a shadow of doubt. In the *Theatre Magazine* for April, 1903, appeared an article entitled "The Negro on the Stage," by an anonymous author. It said, in part, "Bert Williams has long enjoyed the reputation of being a vastly funnier man than any white comedian now on the American stage. He is spontaneously and genuinely humorous, he is not only a funny man, he can act. Those who know what Williams can do are convinced that in a part combining comedy and pathos, this colored thespian would score a great triumph, and soon attain as prominent a place on the dramatic stage as Booker T. Washington on the political."[13]

His acting in "Lode of Kole" in 1909, followed by a ten-year engagement in "Ziegfeld Follies," is sufficient evidence of his popularity.[14] The aspiration of Williams to appear in drama more serious than that of caricature is observed in David Belasco's introduction to "The Son of Laughter," a biography of Bert Williams, in which the impresario writes, "Bert Williams' death probably prevented his appearing under my direction as a star. Negro drama will always be indebted to the genius of the great comedian, and appreciative of the fact that by breaking into 'The Follies' Bert Williams unlocked the doors of the American theater to later Negro artists."[15]

About this time Joseph S. Cotter was beginning to feel that the American Negro had his educational, political, and economic program all wrong, and that it amounted to nothing.[16] Accordingly, Cotter set

[13] Gregory, *op. cit.*, p. 96.
[14] *Ibid.*, p. 96.
[15] Margaret Roland, *The Son of Laughter*, p. III.
[16] J. S. Cotter, *Caleb, the Degenerate*, 1903. Act III, scene 1.

49

about to satirize the situation in a little play, "Caleb, the Degenerate." This attempted to treat the types, customs, and needs of the Negro. At the very moment, W. E. B. DuBois was taking issue with Booker T. Washington on the assumption that industrial education was an admission of inferiority, and thereby precipitated segregation. With Washington's idea of industrial education in mind plus his personal opinion, Cotter sets up a bishop as a model, advocating industrial training. In Act III, his hero is observed in a high state of ecstasy. He is lounging around in a work shop modernly equipped with anvils, hammers, forges, benches, and shoe repairing tools, and surrounded by a wall lined with completed work of the various departments. Notwithstanding the fact that the hero has desires of seducing his own daughter, he reminds his audience that a naked African is superior to an American Negro collegian. Finally, the piece comes to what is supposed to be a melodramatic climax with a satirical diatribe against higher education and politics among Negroes:

> You are as simple as that conjurer,
> You hold a vote is simple remedy
> For all the ills a backward race may have;
> You must not think of things political.

Aside from musical comedy, this piece immediately suggests that the Negro influence on American drama during the first decade of the twentieth century was indeed negligible.

In the meantime the white propagandists were just as busy in using the stage to counteract any favorable impression the Negro actor or playwright might leave. Thomas Dixon wrote the "Clansman," which was widely read and, produced as a moving picture some years later, added much stimulus to the rapidly increasing Negrophobia. William Vaughn Moody is concerned with the religion of the Negro in "The Faith Healer." "In Pride of Race," Robert Hilliard discussed the terrible bugbear known as miscegenation.

The recognition that Negro actors of serious drama had enjoyed from Sheldon's "The Nigger" was ephemeral, for there was no way the Negro's abilities and talent could get beyond his own immediate realm. Broadway of New York and the Pekin Theatre in Chicago, where Bert Williams, Cole, Johnson and Johnson, and George Walker's wife, Ada, were receiving attention, were the only openings for Negro actors in either the eastern or western direction during those days—between 1900 and 1914. The Chicago *Defender* for May 3, 1930, points out that the lot of the Negro actor was indeed hard, and his path more than unusually difficult. Work was uncertain, and wages more so. On playing to small houses throughout the country, he seldom earned enough for maintenance; consequently, he was forced to telegraph to friends, acquaintances, and relatives for railroad fare. Continuing, the *Defender* states that to those who had the grit to follow it through, and blaze the trail over the footlights in those gloomy days, goes much credit.

SUMMARY

There was a definite break with the minstrel tradition between 1895 and 1914. Several influences were responsible for this departure. Becoming interested in musical comedy and popular songs, Negro composers and playwrights wrote for the New York stage. After the exile of the Negro from the legitimate stage of New York, Negroes in Chicago, New York, and Washington built theatres of their own. Segregation in the South, after the period of Reconstruction, had caused southern Negroes to build separate houses. In the meantime, Sam Jack, Bert Williams, John W. Isham, and Williams and Walker, took seriously to musical comedy.

CHAPTER IV

TOWARD DRAMATIC MUSIC

Despite his inactivity, the Negro's background which had been steeped in drama had developed in the Negro an ease of bodily carriage, a spontaneity of muscles, and a voice of such natural richness that he was destined to become even greater than many of the white masters of the art of drama. But the opportunity for expression seemed slow in arriving. For seven lean years this talent lay dormant. Negro talent was everywhere, with no one possessing sufficient courage to put it before the public.

Nothing illustrates this better than the careers of the Tutt brothers. They began their theatrical career with S. H. Dudley's Smart Set Company in the seasons of 1904, 1905, and 1906. Then they starred with "Black Patti's Troubadors" in 1906 and in 1907. Organizing a smart set company of their own in 1908, they had a successful show which was renamed "Smart Set." The Company disbanded in 1916.

Their versatile minds were of such that they wrote musical comedies, presenting them in all sections of the United States and Canada during the interim. Numbered among their best comedies are "His Excellency, the President," "Three Mayors of Newtown," "George Washington," "My People," presented at the Lexington Theatre, New York City, "Darkest Americans," "Children of the Sun," "Up and Down," "Oh Joy," presented at a theatre on 57th

53

Street, New York City, and "Little Brown Lady."
"Oh Joy" received favorable comment from twenty-
one leading dailies and publications. In addition to
writing and producing high class shows for a number
of years, Salem and Tutt made a specialty of training
actors.

During the summer months they did stock in New-
port News, in Washington, in Baltimore, and in Philadelphia, writing their own shows and doing musical
and dramatic numbers. Their first trip to Broadway
was with one of their regular season shows called "Up
and Down." While they were starred, they featured
some who were later to be great stars; namely, Ethel
Waters, Margaret Simms, Emmett Anthony, and An-
drew Tribble.

The next trip of the Tutt brothers to Broadway was
with "Deep Harlem," in 1929, written by Earl Dancer, with book and lyrics by Tutt and Tutt, and music
by Joe Jordan. In 1930, they joined the "Green Pastures," Salem as "Noah," and Homer as "The Cus-
tard Maker." Two weeks after the show opened Wesley Hill was killed and Homer did "Gabriel." Later
when his brother died in 1934 he did "Noah." In
1937, Homer did the role of "Paw" in "How Come
Lawd." In 1938, he played the leading role of "The
King" in the native African dance drama, "Zun-
guru."[1]

The career of Noble Sissle also showed some effort

[1] Salem Tutt "Whitney" also found time to write a weekly
column in first *The Freeman*, Indianapolis, Ind. For sixteen
years he wrote a weekly column in *The Chicago Defender*,
called "Salem Sez" and "Timely Topics." Also in 1926, he
published a book of poems, *Mellow Musings*, published by The
Colored .Poetic League Of The World, Boston, Mass. *Municipal Court*, Part One. No. 47, West 151st Street, New York,
N. Y.

in this direction. One of the most versatile of Negro characters is Noble Sissle. He succeeds in whatever activities he attempts. At one time he is producer; at another he is actor. He is a well known orchestra leader and at the same time a Harlem successful business man. During the World War, he was drum major of the 369th Regiment. More recently he has been the leader of the orchestra which played on the roof garden of the Park Central Hotel from which he has broadcast many programs over the National Radio System.

When General Gourand, in charge of the French Troops in the Champagne sector, heard Sissle sing "Joan of Arc" to the accompaniment of the hell fighters regimental band, July 4, 1918, Sissle found fame and praise for the first time. On returning to the United States, he assisted in organizing the dramatic company of Sissle and Blake.

The play which distinguished him as a man of dramatic technique was "The Chocolate Dandies." For this production he assembled a group of Harlem singers and dancers who had what he termed "hot feet." Hot, too, must have been his own feet, because he played the leading role. Hearing and reading of the success "Chocolate Dandies" was making in Harlem, managers and critics attended its performances to judge its possibilities as a Broadway production. As a result, the play moved to Broadway where it was a very successful show.

Beginning with light musical numbers, the Negro was soon to be recognized in operatic music. As time went on, the Negro developed more technique in form. In the role of a comic singer, the Negro first appeared on the stage in 1815 in "The Battle of Lake Champlain.'' Occasionally thereafter followed other instances of Negroes thus performing. The full development of the race in this sphere, however, came during recent years. By 1920 the Negro was singing, on the concert stage, the compositions of the great composers.

Between 1900 and 1910 the Theodore Drury Opera Company staged annually a grand opera at the Lexington Opera House. Among those produced were *Carmen, Aida,* and *Faust.* These occasions were great social affairs, and were looked forward to with much interest.

Other persons interested in dramatic music were Samuel Coleridge Taylor, and John T. Layton. The latter won praise in the performance of the Hiawatha trilogy in Washington in 1903. Others included Mrs. Azalia Hackley, a success on the concert stage, and in the production of folk festivals among southern Negroes; Sidney Woodward noted for his performance in "Aida," and compositions of Carmen; Edmund T. Jenkins, who studied at the Royal Academy in London, and was signally honored in 1916 for his ability with the clarinet. Moreover, Clarence Cameron White is composer of such orchestral hits as "Bandanna Sketches," and "From the Cotton Field." His "Ouanga" is a more serious effort based on a Haitian background. Merritt Hedgeman made a definite impression when he appeared at the Brooklyn Academy of Music, September 28, 1939. Lillian Evanti has appeared before the operatic circles of Europe for a number of years. She was, in fact, stranded in South America while on a musical tour, when France declared war on Imperial Germany in 1939.

TOWARD DRAMATIC MUSIC

An unusual performer of considerable dramatic reputation is Catarina Jarboro, who played and sang in musical drama for several years. In 1926, she took a seven-year leave of absence to go to Italy to study under specialists. Appearing as *Aida* at the Puccini Theatre in Milan, she received honorable mention. She returned to the United States in the summer of 1933, and made her American operatic debut with the Chicago Opera Company at the Hippodrome. In the fall of 1934, she made a tour of southern schools and cities, giving performances of *Aida* to unusually appreciative audiences. On a four years' concert and operatic tour throughout Continental Europe and Russia, Miss Jarboro became a celebrated international soprano. Returning to America, she thrilled a capacity audience gathered to hear her sing at the Academy of Music, Brooklyn, New York, October 5, 1939.

The excellent work of Roland Hayes as a tenor, the promise given in Todd Duncan as a baritone, and the artistry shown by Marian Anderson, the contralto with one of the rare voices of the century, indicate what might be the future of the Negro in opera. The rise of Dorothy Maynor adds emphasis to this suggestion. Madame Lillian Evanti's career shows promise in this direction.

Other demonstrations of the Negro's operatic possibilities are not wanting. In October, 1926, Jule Bledsoe made his operatic debut in "Deep River," the scene of which was the Creole section of New Orleans, in 1835. His interpretation of "Voodoo" gave that stage event a distinctly redeeming feature. In it, he played opposite Rose McClendon, who exhibited every earmark of grace, charm, and stage bearing. The grace and deep resonant quality of Mr. Bledsoe's tone

57

in "Deep River" paved the way for his receiving leads in "Show Boat," and Verdi's "Aida," in the summer of 1932. Likewise, he received ovations at the Chicago World's Fair in the summer of 1933. Going immediately to London, he was featured in an opera based on the story of "The Emperor Jones."

On October 10, 1935, at the Alvin Theatre, New York City, "Porgy and Bess," a folk opera, had its premiere. Derived from "Porgy," the play of 1927 by DuBose and Dorothy Heyward, it was set to opera by George Gershwin. Among the players were Todd Duncan, who was borrowed from the Department of Music, Howard University, and who took the leading role, Ann Wiggins Brown, Georgette Harvey, Abbie Mitchell, Warren Coleman, Edward Matthews, Rosamond Johnson and Ruby Elzey.

In the words of Brooks Atkinson of The New York *Times*, "DuBose and Dorothy Heyward wrote the original—but 'Porgy and Bess' represents George Gershwin's longing to compose an American folk opera on a suitable theme. The effort is unmistakably George Gershwin's personal holiday."

There are many who have attested to the merit of the original "Porgy," but the apprehensive question of "Where's my Bess?" and the tender response of "I am on my way," is sufficient indication that the latter production of George Gershwin is a bit more interesting.

As a composer of dramatic music the Negro is not without distinction. The man of the moment is H. Lawrence Freeman, who resides in New York City. He made his operatic venture in September, 1928, with his composition, the *Voodoo*, which was produced at the Fifty-Second Street Theatre. Of the dozen grand

TOWARD DRAMATIC MUSIC

operas which he has composed, the following are most
familiarly known: "Martyr," "The "Prophecy,"
"The Octoroon," "Plantation," and "Vendetta."
He has presented, from time to time, in Steinway Hall,
New York City, scenes from his compositions. These
efforts of Mr. Freeman deserve commendation, despite
their crude spots, because they furnish a new and important type of dramatic literature. He was winner
of the 1929 Harmon Award for musical composition.

Professor William L. Dawson has won distinction
with his symphony at Tuskegee Institute. Taking his
"Negro Folk Symphony" to Philadelphia where it
performed before polite society, Professor Dawson received approbation from Dr. Leopold Stokowski in
November, 1934. During the season of 1933-34 Shirley Graham was called upon to present her musical
Drama, "Tom-Tour," in the Cleveland Municipal
Stadium.

William Grant Still has risen to a still higher level.
He first achieved distinction with his Afro-American
Symphony in 1934. He was honored in being chosen
in 1939 to compose the musical theme of the New York
World's Fair. Grover A. Whalen, the head of the exposition, said that the Fair authorities had spent much
time in selecting a composer for the theme music.
Published and unpublished works of several composers were played on records, without the judges knowing the names of the composers. Finally, it was unani-
mously agreed that the composer of "Lenox Avenue"
and "From a Deserted Plantation" seemed to be most
capable of giving musical expression to the mood and
color of the exhibit.[2]

[2] *Kappa Alpha Psi Journal*, "Music in the World of Tomorrow," October, 1939, p. 10.

Of the theme, Mr. Still says, "It is a symphonic poem with a coral finale. The spectators find themselves cast in the role of Gods of old, 'able from Olympian heights to pierce the fogs of ignorance, habit and prejudice that envelop everyday thinking, able to gaze down on the ideal community that man could build today were he to make full use of his tools, his resources and his knowledge.' "

Music critics consider Still, at the age of 44, as the representative American composer of future years. Their opinion is that he will combine classical music with jazz idiom to create works of authentic American quality. Born in Mississippi to William Grant Still, Sr., and Carrie Lambro Still, young Still soon left for Arkansas, and then to Wilberforce University from which he was dropped because of poor scholarship. In the words of the World's Fair publicity agents, "He squandered his allowance on musical books, which he read in classes, refused to study and had such a poor record that he was finally flunked out of college." Accomplishing his aim, he was later graduated from the Oberlin Conservatory of Music. He subsequently studied at the New England Conservatory for three years.

Still says that Sophie Tucker gave him his first chance to show what he could do. His job with her was orchestrating the music for her acts. He is of the opinion that much of W. C. Handy's "St. Louis Blues" is due to his having worked with Mr. Handy in Memphis. Later he did the orchestrations for Earl Carroll's "Vanities" and "Rain or Shine," the second "Americana," et cetera. Meanwhile, he was arranger for "Deep River Hour" a radio program, and for Paul Whiteman's orchestra. Whiteman author-

ized him to write "From a Deserted Plantation."
He has done work for Warner Brothers and the
Columbia Pictures. For a time, he conducted the Los
Angeles Symphony Orchestra, the Federal Orchestra
in San Francisco, and the San Diego Symphony Orchestra in that city. His other works, in addition to
"Lenox Avenue" originally composed for the Columbia Broadcasting Company, include: "Africo-Ameri-
can Symphony," Symphony in G Minor; "Sahdji,"
an African ballet; "La Guiablesse," a ballet based on
a legend of Martinique, and "Kaintuck," a composition for piano and orchestra.

Not without some merit in dramatic music is Clarence Muse. He was born in Baltimore, Maryland, to
parents of comfortable means. As a school boy he
did odd jobs during vacation and after school. His
father, who was a huckster, enabled him to attend
Dickinson University, a small institution in Pennsylvania. Before getting very far in college his father
died, and he was forced to finish his education by hard
drudgery, quitting not until he was graduated from
law school. Lawrence Ranch rightly thinks that music gained in the loss of law, for he "went to New
York and did bits in plays, all kinds of small roles to
achieve a foothold. He spent many years on the
road."[3]

Before achieving fame, he spent seven lean years
virtually giving his versatile talent to the Lafayette
Theatre in New York; nevertheless, he built a background that has served in good stead ever since. At
this Harlem playhouse, he wrote, acted, composed, arranged and danced. In short, he did every kind of

[3] Lawrence Lee Ranch, *Opportunity*, Triple Threat Artist,
September, 1939, pp. 275-276.

theatrical work to gain his bearing. Inclining toward music, he was soon to become a specialist. Lovers of popular music will not soon forget that he wrote "When It's Sleepy Time Down South," which literally became a national theme song. He also struck a sincere and popular note when he wrote "Behind the Cabin Door."

Noted for his flair for music, he has been an actor and writer of imagination of generally artistic calibre. At the Lafayette Theatre, where he served his apprenticeship, he satiated those who liked the high-brow flavor of Shakespeare and Stevenson as well as those who found enjoyment in popular comedy.

Hollywood officials heard him do spirituals on radio programs and promptly sent for him. There, he remained. With an all-colored company, he produced "Porgy" at the Hollywood Music Box.[4] Making the most of his spare time, he directed the 170 voices that sang in "Run Little Chillun," a Los Angeles Federal Theatre production. The Philharmonic Symphony Orchestra of Los Angeles performed his "Harlem Heav'n." The Detroit Symphony Orchestra delighted several audiences with it, and radio programs also featured it.[5]

We see something of the drama also in the man who is behind the scenes of "Hot Mikado" and the Radio City Music Hall, Charles L. Cook. A native of Detroit, he became famous in Chicago with a jazz band called "Doc Cook and His Fourteen Doctors of Syncopation." He has been with the Radio City Music Hall since its beginning, doing orchestrations for Erno Rapee, head of the music staff. For six years he

[4] Ranch, *op. cit.*, p. 275.
[5] Stated in a personal letter from Mr. Muse.

composed music for the Remick Music Company. Before doing the music for the "Brown Buddies," he had arranged overtures for the R. K. O. circuit. Perhaps his greatest claim to fame came when he translated the traditional music of Gilbert and Sullivan into modern tempos. With a staff of ten assistants, he did this Herculean task in four weeks. For a number of years he has been considered an outstanding arranger and composer, often collaborating with such luminaries as Abe Olman, Gus Kahn and Walter Donaldson.

Summary

Even more popular than the light music, has been the Negro's contribution to the concert stage. In addition to having written folk symphony, the Negro has achieved notice as an operatic singer. Nathaniel Dett, H. Lawrence Freeman, and William Grant Still have been successful as writers, while Roland Hayes, Marian Anderson, Catherine Jarboro, Lillian Evanti, Dorothy Maynor and Todd Duncan have distinguished themselves as interpreters of concert music.

CHAPTER V

NEGRO THEMES BY WHITE AUTHORS

Writing in 1926, David Belasco stated:[1] "The theatre of tomorrow must reckon with a new force, the race of Ham. The Negro from today onward will compel recognition through the sheer power of his intrinsic mine of talent. No race can surpass the Negro for his instinctive stage ability. He is a natural actor with a sufficient background of tragedy to make him fertile ground." Serious drama of the Negro, however, was not produced on the New York stage until Edward Sheldon introduced a new theme. Other plays dealing with life and character of the Negro followed, culminating in Marcus Connelly's "The Green Pastures." The Negro as a dramatic theme has supplied the playwright with a wealth of material for drama.

The best production during the first decade of the twentieth century is attributed to Edward Sheldon. He was born in Chicago, and spent his early youth there in a family of playwrights. Recognizing in the Negro the gift of temperament and dramatic instinct, he wrote "The Nigger." The nature of its treatment and its material will be remembered as a significant improvement on earlier attempts dealing with Negro themes.

The plot deals with Governor Philip Morrow, a

[1] David Belasco, "Theatre of Tomorrow," *The Literary Digest*, August 7, 1926, p. 219.

young southerner, who has been elected to his office
as an advocate of white supremacy. He is shockingly
surprised on learning that he is the grandson of a
Negro slave. The disclosure is all the more dramatic
when the governor's cousin, a bootlegger, reveals the
information, after forcing the governor to veto a prohibition bill. The cousin, Noyes by name, has found
a letter written years before by Belle, a slave mistress
to the governor's grandfather. In the letter, she
writes affectionately, bidding the governor God-speed
before she is sold down the river.

Sheldon was congratulated for two reasons: in
the first place, because of his courage; and, in the second place, because of his clever handling of his material. Having Belle write a letter and subtly intro-
ducing it as a means of unraveling the plot is a distinct bit of drama, only to be climaxed with the presence of Jenny, Belle's sister, who, although in the
home of the family, has retained the letter for seventy
years.

Ridgely Torrence conceived the idea that he, too,
would try his hand at the racial art. Impressed with
that idea, early in 1917, he wrote three one-act plays:
"Granny Maumee," "Simon the Cyrenian," and the
"Rider of Dreams," the last more popularly known
in Negro circles than either of the former two. The
author of this play has brought to the fore one of
the more glaring realities of southern custom—abuse
of Negroes by lawless whites. As the plot begins to
unravel, one observes a hard-working woman striving
to make her son a useful citizen, by sending him to
school, and helping the husband and father to pur-
chase a home that would enhance their security and
stability, only to see her golden ambitions and efforts

reduced to naught, because her husband has become a victim of a dishonest white man who has taken advantage of the Negro's dreams.

So much did these plays impress Mrs. Norman Hapgood that she produced them on April 5, 1917. Dramatic critics who witnessed the production of the plays were disposed to feel that if it had not been for the American declaration of war on Imperial Germany the following day, the staging of those plays would have had a successful outcome under the able direction of Mrs. Hapgood. Be that as it may, the effort of Mrs. Hapgood was deserving of serious and favorable consideration.

Theretofore, the impression that people had of the Negro, on stage and off, was what they had gleaned from minstrelsy and fantastic comedy, which was often only the debased and vitiated life. In the portrayal of this aspect of Negro life and character, that is, the giving up of money to its rightful owner, and a lecture by a man of vision and insight, much material was furnished for critical comment.

Though the plays are not entirely free from literary crudeness, they present native attributes. Opal Cooper, who played the leading male role in "Rider of Dreams," interpreted that role so admirably that it resulted in his being cast in subsequent important productions. Had the production done little more than to focus public attention upon Inez Clough, who ably supported Cooper, that fact alone would have more than merited its expenditures.

Carl Van Vechten, author of "Nigger Heaven," who covered the production made this interesting observation in the *Literary Digest*: "Heretofore resident companies did not present Negro drama because

66

there was none.'' Mr. Van Vechten was particularly moved by the stirring drama of ''Granny Maumee,'' the scene of which is a Negro hut in the deep South, near which Granny's son has been lynched for a crime committed by a white man. In attempting to protect her son, the devoted mother is also burned at the stake. With a stroke of dramatic subtlety, Torrence cleverly introduces the child's father, who is also the father of the perpetrator of the crime. In so doing, Torrence shows himself a dramatist above the ordinary.

Meanwhile, Eugene O'Neill had been a student at Princeton and Harvard Universities, studying under Professor Baker at the latter institution. He was confident that the Negro had potential dramatic qualities which, if developed and encouraged, would bestow honor and credit upon those who would bring out those qualities.[2]

O'Neill began with a little play, ''The Moon of the

[2] Commenting on ''The Emperor Jones,'' O'Neill's masterpiece, and Gilpin, the star, the New York *Herald Tribune* said on May 10, 1930: ''Charles Gilpin, one of America's great actors is dead, and he will be remembered for a single role. Those who saw him play the title-role in 'The Emperor Jones' will never forget him, and his magnificent interpretation of that part has had much to do with the sudden rise to world fame of Eugene O'Neill. Gilpin was on and off the stage from the time he was 15, until he was 50, but he found it more profitable to be a pullman porter, a barber, or a chicken farmer. He appeared on Broadway only twice, first as William Curtis in John Drinkwater's 'Abraham Lincoln.' Gilpin's playing of that part of the porter, turned Emperor, stumbling through the tropic forest, made Macdougal Street for the moment the theatrical mecca of New York. Finally the play had to move to Broadway, and despite dire predictions, succeeded on the large uptown stage as well as in Greenwich Village. In 1921 it was inevitable that the Drama League should count Gilpin as among the ten persons who had contributed most to dramatic art during the year. The actor who was 57 years old sought to regain his health by operating a small chicken farm, but his health failed steadily, resulting in death.''

Caribbean.'' The scene is laid in the West Indies, on board a ship, with a cast consisting of natives. The Provincetown Players produced that one-act piece at the Provincetown Playhouse in November, 1918. While the venture was small, and aroused only passing attention, it gave O'Neill a cue. Forthwith, O'Neill came out with ''Dreamy Kid,'' another one-act play, dealing with Negro character and life, making its New York premiere at the Provincetown Playhouse, October 31, 1919.[3] Since that time Negro theatres, churches, and schools throughout the country have had the ''Dreamy Kid'' on their programs time and again.

The setting takes place in a Negro settlement in contemporary New York in the bedroom of Mammy Saunders who is on the brink of death. Although greatly comforted by Celia Ann, her final wish is to see Abbie, the dreamy kid, before she passes on. The conflicting factors become all the more serious when the boy arrives, revealing that he has slain a white man who had threatened to kill him. The scene becomes touching and pathetic as life slowly ebbs from the body of Mammy, with Abbie holding her hand, swearing that the police will not take him alive. He is ready to leap any second, spilling blood in his getaway, should the officers attempt to corner him.

Within the limits of this story, O'Neill brought out a very significant social revelation. A Negro has killed a white man, but as he says, ''Twarn't my doing no how. He was the one looking for trouble. He told de folks dat he was going to get me, and dat forced my hand.'' Evidently this was a mat-

[3] Sterling Brown, Negro Character as Seen by White Authors. *Journal of Negro Education*, April, 1933, p. 196.

ter of self-defense on the part of the "Kid." It
also shows, among other things, the Negro's distrust
for law and "justice." By a subtle stroke, O'Neill
demonstrates how the Negro is compelled to take the
law into his own hands as a means of protection.

As previously stated, the piece caught the fancy of
play-lovers. With renewed inspiration, having sought
and found dramatic material in the Negro, O'Neill no
longer believed that the American public would refuse
to patronize Negro productions.

With the foregoing belief in mind, O'Neill went to
work on a drama incomparable to anything dealing
with Negro drama since "Othello." And on November 3, 1920, the curtain rose on "The Emperor Jones"
at the Playhouse in Greenwich Village, New York,
with Charles Gilpin in the title-role. As The New York
Herald pointed out on the death of Gilpin,[4] it was the
play that made both actor and playwright famous. It
was a fine production, and the audiences did not need
critics to verify their convictions. Those who saw the
production still regard it as having been written and
acted by artists. It is small wonder, therefore, that
the Drama League voted Gilpin one of the ten who had
made the best contribution to the theatre of that year
and that he was invited to a dinner in honor of the
ten thus honorably mentioned. News of the dinner
created no little amount of racial friction, unrest and
nasty comment, precipitated, for the most part, by
the Hearst syndicate. Notwithstanding the criticism,
the Drama League was unyielding for the sake of its
art.

This drama[5] is the story of an ignorant, supersti-

[4] *Herald Tribune*, May 10, 1930.
[5] F. W. Bond, *Speech Construction*. Boston: The Christopher Publishing House, 1936, p. 82.

tious pullman porter whose rise to influence, prestige and power is immediately followed by a sudden fall from his lofty height, terminating in death. The conflicting factor at work in this highly dramatic piece is Jones' ambition for power. Terror, however, is an important feature in the development of the story. So dramatically and forcefully is this terror described in the eighth scene that the reader and observer, on first reaction, sympathize with the Emperor. It is not surprising, therefore, that Smithers says of him, "E's better man than the lot o' you put together. I 'ates the sight of 'im, but I'll say that for 'im." There is, too, the superstition of the natives, coupled with ignorance and fear. Jones, whose ambition rules for awhile, is in command, but when the natives are severely taxed they desert him, and his empire comes tumbling down, like a house built on sand.

The reason for Jones' being thousands of miles from his native Southland is that he is a fugitive from justice. He is a murderer, having killed a man in a card game. As a consequence, he is a hardened man, estranged from his native land. This is revealed to the reader through the dialogue when the Emperor and Smithers talk in the deserted palace, and again when Jones, lost in the forest, asks Jesus to forgive him for all the crimes he has committed . . . .

The story opens in the palace of the Emperor, who, at the time, is fast asleep. Smithers, a white trader, and supposed friend of the Emperor, is bemoaning the fact that the ragged Negro he had befriended has turned the isle upside down in the brief period of two years. The Emperor has the natives believing that he is God, and that only a silver bullet will kill him.

NEGRO THEMES BY WHITE AUTHORS

When the last man has deserted him, the Emperor betakes himself to foreign fields in order to enjoy the money he has exacted from the poor natives. During his flight in the night, he has strange hallucinations, and sees apparitions that cause him to fall into hysterics. He suffers a strange dementia.

Lem, an old African Negro, trails the Emperor with Smithers, who, for the sake of his own hide, and for his own greed, wants the simple Emperor annihilated; whereupon the soldiers make a silver bullet and kill Jones.

O'Neill's style is vivid, forceful and entertaining. His Negro dialect is nearly perfect, and is steeped in realism and wit. It is dynamic, human, and characteristic of the person it endeavors to portray. The dramatist's scenes add flavor to the play, and help O'Neill to show his main character at his best.

Jones is cunning, revengeful, fearful, sarcastic, superstitious, self-confident, conceited, childish, simple, hateful, desperate, but religious. Unfortunately, Jones is his own worst enemy, for he is a victim of his own conceit, and over-confidence.

Smithers, the only white man in the play, is a type that the better class of his race avoid. He is known to be conceited, jealous, unreliable, subtle, haughty, rapacious, and always suspicious. He hates Jones in life but reveres him in death.

O'Neill's next venture in Negro drama was the writing of "All God's Chillun Got Wings." It had its premiere at the Provincetown Playhouse, May 15, 1924, with Paul Robeson in the title-role. Assuming that the modern audience was still interested in Negro drama, he wrote for their entertainment this stirring play, featuring the miseries of Jim Harris, who married Ella Downey, a white woman of inferior character and stock. For reasons not definitely known to students of the stage, the Mayor of the City of New York prevented the appearance of children in the first scene, a scene that shows that race prejudice does not enter the mind of children. The Mayor's office may have been influenced by unpleasant propaganda, or it may have felt that it was a bit too unusual to permit a colored boy to carry a white girl's books to school, which kindness on the boy's part precipitated admiration for the lad, because of his large muscles, and masculine charm. He was so intelligent, so masculine, so robust, so superior in scholarship and extra-curricular activities that increased admiration followed, and culminated in marriage. Thrown, however, into a society that does not condone intermarriage, dreadful consequences immediately overtook them.

In constructing the plot of this couple, O'Neill has shown distinct dramatic art. With dextrous dramatization, he goes about the task of compelling the reader and playgoer to wonder how and why did such a fine fellow as Jim get tied up with such a terribly wicked woman, who was the rejected harlot of a pugilist. No doubt thinking at this point that public opinion would be most indignant at the very thought of intermarriage, O'Neill went so far that he leaned backwards, making his heroine fit only for a mental ward. Unlike Othello's charming and ever appreciative Desdemona, this licentious creature was a thorn in the side of Jim. His ambition to become a lawyer failed to materialize because of his spouse's indifference, and lack of wifely interest.

When the play opened at the Provincetown Playhouse, May 6, 1924, the delicate role of Afro-husband was taken over by a person who had the exact qualities which O'Neill had in mind when he created Jim Harris' role. This person was Paul Robeson, a four-letter man, Phi Beta Kappa, and football star from Rutgers, and a product of the Columbia University Law School.[6] Mary Blair, a talented actress, did the role of the white maniac. It is said that she suffered pitiably in that concluding despicable scene in which she had to appear diseased of mind. In the opinion of the old New York *Telegram*, "It is one of the most appealing moral plays that has ever been presented in a theatre, and it is intensely dramatic."[7] Be that as it may, the play at least proves one point conclusively: that the Negro had come a long way up the dramatic ladder, demonstrating, as he came, the vicissitudes of his race.

For Robeson's performance in this production, George Jean Nathan wrote in part:

"The singularly fine performance of the role of Jim Harris that the Negro Robeson gave recently in Eugene O'Neill's 'All God's Chillun' brings still further positive testing to the theory that the black man is far better fitted naturally for the profession of acting than his white brothers . . . The Negro is a born actor, where the white man achieves acting. Robeson, with relatively little experience, and with no training to speak of, is one of the most thoroughly eloquent, impressive and convincing actors that I have looked at and listened to in the past twenty years of theatre-going. As to his Negro colleague, Gilpin here acts with all the unrestrained and terrible sincerity of which the white actor, save on rare occasions, is by virtue of his shellac of civilization just a trifle ashamed."[8]

[6] E. G. Robeson, *Paul Robeson, Negro.* London, 1930, pp. 27-39.
[7] The New York *Telegram*, May 7, 1924.
[8] George Jean Nathan, *The American Mercury*, July, 1924, pp. 371-372.

THE NEGRO AND THE DRAMA

After his performance in "All God's Chillun Got Wings," the old New York *World* said of Robeson:

"He played the role Charles Gilpin, another Negro, had created in 'The Emperor Jones.' A great many competent judges have said that he rose to power and dignity over-powering Gilpin's. Now in the present play there is no doubt about his ability—ability in appreciation to Robeson's work as the Negro in 'All God's Chillun Got Wings.' The man brings genius to the piece. What other player on the American stage has his great taut body—the swinging grace and lightness of the man who with a football under his arm sidestepped half the broken field of the East?"[9]

In the introduction to *Paul Robeson*, Eugene O'Neill wrote:

"In gratitude to Paul Robeson in whose interpretation of Brutus Jones, I have found the most complete satisfaction any author can get—that of seeing his creation born into flesh and blood, and in whose creation of Jim Harris in my 'All God's Chillun Got Wings' I have found not only complete fidelity to my intent under trying circumstances, but beyond that, true understanding and racial integrity."[10]

Another playwright in this same field, Paul Green, professor in the University of North Carolina, also made himself widely known. After he had written "Last of the Lowries" (1920) he seriously delved into Negro material as themes for his plays. During the same year in which he wrote this play he produced "White Dresses."

The scenes of "White Dresses" is a Negro home in North Carolina, a few days before Christmas. Granny McLean, an elderly colored woman, whose days here are few, is trying to make herself comfortable in a comfortless room, meanwhile keenly concerned about her granddaughter, Mary, who is away working for a white family, the Morgans. Presently, Mary returns

[9] New York *World*, June 21, 1924.
[10] Robeson, *op. cit.*, p. 111.

74

with a variety of presents, presumably from Morgan. Greatly perturbed, Granny now comes to life, and reveals a shockingly tragic story. She begins her exhortation by severely admonishing Mary against accepting favors or gifts from Morgan. Then, with disgust, she opens a small box from which she takes a white dress similar to the one which Morgan has given Mary for Christmas. So angry does she become, that she thrusts both into the fire, at the same time reminding Mary of the incident in connection with the dress a white man had given her 19 years ago. Here Green suavely unfolds the fact that this white man desires to seduce his own daughter, Mary, making advances to her in the same manner that he had to Mary's mother.

That this is American life in the raw, Green courageously portrays. Among other things, the play shows that all moral restrictions, all social standards are broken down by this type of social behavior. The author seems greatly moved by the effect it has made on American society. He emphasizes in that final horrid scene, that this is truly one of the more glaring realities of American life and character.

Paul Green's drama entitled "In Abraham's Bosom" (1920) is the story of turpentine hands in North Carolina. The action takes place at noon in the woods. Four hands have come to eat their midday meal. Innocently, they talk about many insignificant things. On Missing Abraham, the thought of his whereabouts suddenly flashes into the mind of McGranie, the master. Abraham, being aspiring, ambitious, and serious, desires to lift himself above his environment. In his steadfast determination to improve himself, he brings books to the woods daily, solving problems in his spare moments. The other three hands do not approve of his ambition. Out of pure jealousy, they reveal that Abraham has been decidedly displeased about the recent lynching of another Negro. What is actually more disturbing, however, is that Abraham wants to establish a school for colored children. In short, he wants to develop himself and his race. Because of such an exalted ambition his co-workers feel rather chagrined and irritated; his white boss feels even more vexed and disquieted.

Instead of spending the lunch hour aimlessly with the three other fellows, Abraham climbs a tree to solve arithmetical problems. By the time he begins to concentrate, he is interrupted by Colonel McGranie and his son, Lonnie, who decide that the time can better be spent working. During the interim, Abraham inquires of the Colonel his plans for the proposed school. Without being able successfully to evade the issue, Lonnie intervenes, striking Abraham with a terrific blow. At this stage of developments Green skilfully weaves into the story a very interestingly social feature. He shows Abraham resenting the way his father, the Colonel, treats him. But the father cares not to suffer such indignities from his illegitimate son, and becomes so infuriated with Abraham that he thrashes Abraham unmercifully.

This realistic play of Negro life with its setting in North Carolina in the 1890's was produced at the Provincetown Playhouse December 28, 1926, starring the late Rose McGlendon, Abbie Mitchell, Jules Bledsoe, and Frank Wilson. Green's gripping tale, and dramatic technique, together with incredible interpretation by these stars immediately brought the University of North Carolina professor into national limelight. It was the hit of the season. In fact, it was the play of the year, and brought to its author the Pulitzer Prize.[11]

Continuing his observation of the relationship that exists between white men and colored women, Paul Green has written "The Good Bye" and "The End of the Row." In the first play, Green's theme concerns itself with a man and woman who have been cohabiting for at least eight years. Finally, the white man decides to marry his mistress so that she and their child may legally inherit his money and name. In the second play, the civic-minded heroine has aspirations of improving her community. A white man encourages her ambitions by letting her have the necessary money; selfishly, of course, for he has desires of violating her. In dramatizing this tragic chapter of southern life, Paul Green has taken a bold stroke. Everybody knows, but few are willing to admit, that colored women, in their dilemma, succumb to the animal nature of white men. Though fresh moving drama, these two plays are too weak for eastern producers, too close to the life of southern producers and too rank for amateurs.

"The Prayer Meeting," "The Man Who Died at Twelve o'Clock," "In Aunt Mahaly's Cabin," and "The Hot Iron" deal with the sub-stratum Negro of North Carolina. Submerged in superstition, poverty, suffering and ignorance, the characters of these plays unlike those of the "White Dresses" type are hampered by the forces of nature. The author points out in "The Prayer Meeting" that such ceremonies are not always places in which Negroes worship. They may, as in the case of Granny Boling's grandchildren,

[11] The New York *Sun*, May 1, 1928.

use these meetings to practice free love. The result is tragic, however, for one of the visiting seducers is shot by the girl he has disgraced. "The Man Who Died at Twelve o'Clock" has in it a shiftless scoundrel who upbraids his granddaughter for desiring to marry a local boy. Superstition has its play when the girl reminds her grandfather that he is to die at twelve o'clock. "Hot Iron" is typical of thousands of Negro mothers who have to iron incessantly to support their children whose father she has slain because of his cruel treatment.

Green's second most popular play is "The No 'Count Boy," which appeared in 1924. Although it was not received with as much popular favor as his "In Abraham's Bosom," it has a decided comedy. There is no estimate as to how many children and adults have laughed heartily over the antics of the lazy, easy-going, shiftless, nonchalant, good-for-nothing colored brat, the no-'count-boy.

In this piece, the playwright has again drawn from a rich background of local tradition, as experienced by Negroes of North Carolina, who hope, pray, and long to enjoy the pleasures of life, but never quite attain them. The story is that of a dressed-up country boy, with his beautiful, mulatto girl, who is by no means enthusiastic over her dark beau, whose attempt to make an impression by driving to her shack in his master's buggy to take her for a "small drive before church begun," is delightful comedy. The circumstances take a sudden turn in favor of the no-'count-boy, who gets a chance to talk to Pheelie. In a conversation interspersed with waggish dancing and singing, he tells her of all the great things he has seen: rivers, cities, rich men and women, tall buildings, street cars and automobiles. All these things make a

striking appeal to Pheelie, who decides to run away
with the boy, only to be thwarted by Enos, her original lover, and by the boy's own mammy, who severely
drubs him for being away from home and for lying.

That Green and O'Neill are really great dramatists,
students of the field do not deny. Neither do they
deny that the prestige of these two stage-craftsmen has
been influenced by two equally great actors—Charles
Gilpin and Paul Robeson.

After seeing the performances of each of these actors, Stark Young had occasion to write:

"When the players are Negroes, we are sure to hear from
one quarter or another that there is remarkable action to be
seen. People who shine by discovering an instance of new-
ness which is great art at last, hasten to trumpet the new
greatness of the new real artness. Gilpin developed slowly
and poorly into a certain amount of skill. Paul Robeson
of the same play ('The Emperor Jones') is no actor at all.
Negroes are by nature a superb acting medium. They have
voices that are engaging . . . . and that are theatrical because they are moving, warm and flexible. They have flexible bodies and perfect relaxation, and quick emotional response. American material is flat, while this is new and
live. You see something honest and true."[12]

SUMMARY

Although these writers have not concerned themselves with genuinely artistic productions, they have,
in spite of themselves, brought to the fore actors of
exceptional talent. Beginning at first, in an experimental manner, they were soon to realize that the
Negro, as histrionic material, possessed intrinsic
merit. The efforts of these writers also discarded the
assumption that entertainment of the Negro was
hardly more than caricature of the drollery specie.

[12] Stark Young, ''Material in the Theatre,'' *New Republic*,
May 11, 1927, pp. 331-32.

CHAPTER VI

OTHER WHITE PLAYWRIGHTS WITH NEGRO PLAYERS

In 1923 Leon Gordon, author of "The Piker," "The Garden of Weeds," and "Trade Winds," wrote "White Cargo," a piece dealing with Afro-primitives, that was subsequently produced in New York City. This African study led observers to compare the author of the production with Kipling, Conrad, Green and O'Neill.

The next interesting play, "Lula Belle," was produced by David Belasco, at his own theatre in New York City, March, 1926.[1] A sardonic story of Negro life is this drama of Edward Sheldon, who focused attention on Negro theme in 1909, with his "The Nigger." Digressing from his earlier effort, Sheldon presents a narrative of a colored boy of the Elite Grotto of Harlem, the Negro's haven, tracing him across the ocean to Paris.

So much in love is the young colored man with the maiden that long before he leaves New York, he presents her with pearls for her olive-skin neck; gives her servants that bow at her beck and call; flowers that fill every corner of her boudoir, and perfume that saturates the air about her. Going to Paris to be with his Lula Belle, he begs her to accept his attention, only to be spit upon, again and again. The discarded man becomes so incensed at her rejection of him that he strangles her, even though he is observed a moment

[1] Hubert Harrison, The Significance of "Lula Bell." *The Opportunity Magazine.* May, 1926, p. 258.

later weeping in a state of tangled confusion and remorse.

After several weeks of effort, Belasco organized a well trained troup for "Lula Belle." As stated in the old New York *World*, "The performance is better on that account. By this stroke of casting, he reaps a rich reward in the right flavor which all the scenes of tumult and jubilation have in particular, that of the panoramic first act, when the scenes in pool of light on a 'San Juan' street corner are played to a gibbering, hooting accompaniment from the old crones who brood over the play."[2]

The premiere of "Black Boy," a realistic play in three acts, by James Tully and Frank Dazey, took place at the Comedy Theatre, New York City, October 6, 1926. The story took for its theme pugilism, with Paul Robeson in the title-role. For two years, the black boy was successful and lived a riotous life, but immediately fell from his lofty height when his money ran short.

Without plot, structure, or picturesque story, the play, nevertheless, had sporadic instances of vigor, and freshness, as Robeson gradually settled down to do the task chosen for him.[3] Though a braggart, he proved to be a champion in the prize-ring. Whether Robeson was unfortunately cast, it is not the point here to discuss; the fact remains that his reputation was not enhanced as an actor in "Black Boy."

On March 9, 1927, another play, "Earth," by Em Jo Basshe, had its premiere at the Fifty-Second Street Theatre, New York City. It was a very gripping production and, according to press reports, every scene and incident advanced its story and dramatic move-

[2] The New York *World*, March 10, 1926.
[3] The New York *Age*, October 8, 1926.

ment. Each episode and passage made the audience eager to know what was coming next.

Despite the fact that the theme is concerned with Negro problems, its conclusion is peaceful with a sense of cheerfulness and satisfaction. In the play there is little to cause the reader or audience to disagree with the author's point of view. The piece succeeds in making injustice seem less odious, and virtue triumph over wickedness. One is left to feel on reading the piece that the moral tone is high, and that the lines are bright and refreshing.

Out of "Porgy," by Du Bose and Dorothy Heyward, who became immediately famous with their novel, came a dramatization in 1927. It was one of the sensational dramas of the post-War period, having appeared at a time when the literati of New York were deeply moved by Van Vechten's "Nigger Heaven." Moreover, it was a piece of undoubted dramatic skill.

The narrative is that of the lowest type of Negroes of Charleston, South Carolina, with Porgy, a crippled beggar, as the hero, a familiar character in King Street. Having lived in South Carolina most of his life, Du Bose Heyward felt that his impressions of the Negro should be recorded. He was even more desirous of recording life situations about him when he read in the Charleston *News and Observer* the following:

"Samuel Smalls (Porgy), who is a cripple and is familiar to King Street with his goat and cart, was held for the June term of court of sessions on an aggravated assault charge. It is alleged that on Saturday night he attempted to shoot Maggie Barnes at number four Romney Street. His shots went wide of the mark. Smalls was up on a similar charge some months ago and was given a suspended sentence."[4]

[4] Du Bose Heyward, *Porgy*, London: Boulverie House, 1929, p. xi.

Believing that this tragic figure could never lift himself above his commonplace environment, Heyward set about to put the story before the public at large. And the Theatre Guild of New York City helped him to realize the ambition.

Upon deciding to produce the play, the Theatre Guild chose Cleon Throckmorton, a native southerner, to design the scenery, sending him to Charleston to get first hand information of the setting. Rouben Mamoulian, an Armenian, trained in the Moscow Art Theatre, was selected as director.

Of the characters chosen for the leading roles, Heyward writes:

"The hero of my novel has been a gaunt, tragic figure such as I had often seen on the Charleston water-front. The part was given to Evelyn Ellis, young, slender, and immediately noticeable for a certain radiant charm. Frank Wilson, whose work in 'In Abraham's Bosom' had thrilled us by his emotional power . . . Georgette Harvey was a reincarnation of Maria. Rose McClendon was perfect as the Catfish Row aristocrat, Serena; Richard J. Huey was born for Mingo, and Dorothy Paul for Lily."[5]

Strangely enough, Leigh Whipper was not only actor, but co-playwright of the piece. Having spent his youth in Charleston, he was familiar with what Heyward was striving for. Accordingly, he introduced himself to the Heywards as a fellow Charlestonian. Then, in the words of Heyward, he not only helped to "check the atmosphere of the play," but was also responsible for the bringing into the play the old crab vendor who had been a figure about the streets years ago.[6] After he had depicted the vendor

[5] Heyward, *op. cit.*, pp. 12-13.
[6] *Ibid.*, p. xviii.

to the Heywards, they told him, "Go ahead and put him in Catfish Row."

This play had been made a success largely by the fine acting of Rose McClendon. She passed most of her life in drama and the theatre. She was known on Broadway as the Negro race's first lady. This modest woman often stated that she was far from being a great actress, and that her dramatic success had come quite undeservedly, despite the praise of New York critics. In a conversation with Alexander Woolcott, Ethel Barrymore paid Rose McClendon one of her greatest compliments. On seeing the colored actress walk down the stairs in "Porgy," Miss Barrymore said that she would give anything she possessed just to be able to descend a stairway in that fashion. Other notable productions in which she appeared were "Deep River," "Rose Marie," "In Abraham's Bosom," and "Mulatto."

One of the few recent attempts, by observant white playwrights, to dramatize the upper-class of Negro life was with the production of "Make Me Know It," which had its premiere at the New Rochelle Theatre, New Rochelle, New York, November 2, 1929. This drama by D. Frank Marcus is a distinct piece of stage technique, and presented by a strong cast from New York City, with Barrington Guy, and the late Vivienne Barber in the leading roles. Another creditable character was A. B. Comathiere, fairly fresh from "Porgy." Barrington Guy had made a name for himself in Lew Leslie's "Black Birds." Moreover, he was playing the role of Othello in an amateur production at the same time.

Aubrey Graves of the New York *Telegram* reported that " 'Make Me Know It' is the best all-colored show

I have seen on the stage.'"[7] The New Haven *Times*
was also loud in its praise. After a week's engagement in New Rochelle, the play was taken to the Central Opera House, New York City, where it had a two-
weeks' run.

At the Liberty Theatre, October 7, 1930, "Brown
Buddies," a musical comedy, featuring Bill Robinson
and Adelaide Hall, began a short but fair run. This
play of two acts and eight scenes was enlivened by a
musical monologue which interspersed the excellent
dancing of Miss Hall and Robinson. It was another
production displaying Robinson's rhythmic perfection
in dancing that moved the audience to acclaim. On
this occasion the idol of the dancing art tap-danced
up and down a flight of stairs with as little effort as
if he were on a level floor. And when his feet all but
spoke their meaning, he smiled in recognition of the
audience's approval.[8]

Julia Peterkin's "Scarlet Sister Mary," although
a success as a novel, was taken up by the craft. But
when Ethel Barrymore, in the title-role attempted to
adapt the story to the stage it was unsuccessful. That
it was not successful, seems to surprise none. Based
on the remotest sections of South Carolina, treating
of a tribe of Negroes known as Gullahs, and the illegitimate bearing of babies, it could not by any stretch
of the imagination sustain the interest of Broadway
theatre-goers. When the play opened, November 25,
1930, press reports referred to it as an almost unbe-
lievably trashy play dramatized from a downright
silly novel.[9]

[7] The New York *Telegram*, November 3, 1929.
[8] The New York *Daily News*, October 8, 1930.
[9] The New York *Sun*, November 26, 1930.

Next came "Black Souls," a play which takes the
South as its locale, also the Negro problem as its theme.
It is a play in six scenes, by Miss Annie Nathan. The
play had a short run at the Provincetown Playhouse
in May, 1932. What the play lacked in action, it,
nevertheless, compensated for by the earnest pleadings
of an oppressed group who had been moved by the
recent lynchings of their southern brethren. Such,
was the opinion of Wilella Waldorf, who reviewed it
for the New York *Post*.[10]

The scene of the play is laid in a southern Negro college. The author of the piece seems to have
disagreed with the philosophy of white southerners
who readily admit that Negroes should have industrial
education, but that if Negroes assume that they will
be on an equal basis with the whites upon receiving
professional training, they are very much mistaken.

Though often speaking in platitudes, the governor
is not indefinite when he says, "We are banded together in a great cause—that of maintaining the supremacy of the white race." The governor disregards
the fact that he has been violating the wife of the
college president.

Arriving at the climax of the story, one observes a
senator's daughter, who, while on a mission to France
during the Great War, had fallen in love with a soldier who is now professor at the Institution. Despite
the admonition of the soldier who had turned poet and
professor, the precocious girl insisted upon clandestine
affairs which resulted in a lynching.

The foregoing scene lays the basis for the one that
follows—that of a bitter speech which suggests that
Negroes are all right fighting for their country, but

[10] The New York *Post*, May 3, 1932.

when it comes to social equality, they are decidedly off color.

The piece comes to a startling ending when the college president awakens to the fact that a white man of high office and station has been paying marked attention to his wife. For reasons which the author fails to reveal, the president refuses to make an issue of the revelation, dismissing the affair on the "assumption" that to do otherwise would reflect unfavorably upon his school and his race.

Although innumerable criticisms have been made concerning the famous Scottsboro case, no one seems to have brought out the underlying truth in the case, as has the twenty-seven year old John Wexley, in "They Shall Not Die," which was produced in October, 1933, by the Theatre Guild of New York. Wexley rewrote the Scottsboro trial exactly as it had taken place in Alabama, not even omitting the Lord's prayer, delivered by the New York attorney.

Nine colored boys riding a freight train through the State of Alabama fall upon evil days when they encounter a group of white boys, among whom are two girls. When an embroilment ensues, the white boys are vanquished. Not to be outdone, the whites call the police, accusing the colored boys of raping the girls. Bribed and terrified by the police, the girls corroborate the accusations of the white boys.

"Stevedore," by George Sklar and Paul Peters, two young playwrights, heretofore hardly known to the theatre audience, found in the deep South what ultimately resulted in a striking play. While searching around New Orleans for material, a contrast suddenly flashed in their minds, a social irony, an incident as old as America. The idea had significance, they felt sure. Over it they toiled and brooded, thinking perhaps as George Middleton had thought: that the theme of plays comes from important phases of modern social life.

Believing that a large percentage of "rape cases" are in reality "framed" cases, they set to work to make such a case the core of their plot. Lonnie Thompson, the martyr in this piece, assumes the responsibility of defending his own rights and those of his co-workers. This fact became ultimately the sole reason behind the lynching which followed. Florence Reynolds, a young woman of questionable morals is severely beaten by one of her lovers. The beating brings to the scene her raving husband and bloodthirsty neighbors, who are told that a "nigger" did it. Lonnie and other stevedores of the wharves are arrested, but failing to confess to that which they did not do, even after a third-degree grilling, they are released. Lonnie becomes incensed because of the indignities to which he was subjected, and seeks out the superintendent of docks for a talk in connection with his imprisonment, and his back salary held by the company. In a desperate effort to remove this smart "nigger," lest he poison the minds of other stevedores, the superintendent, though agreeing to give Lonnie his money, strikes him on the jaw with his right fist, and calls the police, reminding them of the rape incident.

Police cruisers are immediately ordered to arrest all suspects. And so "dem cops pick up everybody in sight; they pick 'em off the corner, pull 'em out of the pool room; pull 'em out of the barber shop even. Dey nearly bust in the do' at Jerry's." At the wharf the authors cunningly show how Walcott, the superintendent, points the finger of suspicion at Lonnie, simultaneously making friendly gestures to him. Shouting, cursing, and struggling, Lonnie is dragged off by the police who, indifferently, and without resistance allow a mob of hoodlums to take the prisoner.

"Stevedore," though a Broadway success for the season of 1933-'34, cannot be classed as a work of high order. Its authors did not intend it to be. Having become interested, as thematic material, in the hardships, and drudgery of under-dogs, the playwrights felt that sincerity was their first obligation. Consequently they became deeply interested in their efforts.

The reader has a feeling of pity and admiration for the hero. He addressed himself to the cause of justice. He demanded his rights. New Orleans "justice" hesitated in giving him those rights. Hence, he bravely went about the task demanded of him by those who created his role. He accomplished the point the authors had in mind.

Other Negro characters of the play were far less formidable. Walcott's voice made them cringe. Little gumption did they have, or else they failed to realize that to emerge above one's level of commonplace implies sacrifice, responsibility, or in other words, an attitude similar to that which Lonnie Thompson had.

In its year's run in New York, the play featured in its title-role Jack Carter, whose appearance on the stage was splendid. His actions and reactions did not go beyond proper bounds, and he performed at the crucial moment with dignity. In fact, he became the recipient of unusual commendation and applause.

On April 5, 1934, at the Longacre Theatre, New York City, the curtain rang up on "Brain Sweet,"[11]

[11] The New York *Post*, April 16, 1934.

an unusually humorous comedy. In this skillfully done composition, the producer gathered from Harlem a cast of seasoned comedians who provided much hilarity in their interpretation of Afro-American life.

The story is of Henry Washington, played by Billy Higgins, a pretentious and pompous Negro whose consolations are derived from air castles he builds languishing in a rocking chair while his wife cooks pork chops that she earns by taking in washing. He dreams of what he terms "big ideas," believing he will some day vie with rich men. His chattering continues until his sister-in-law, played by Pearl Wright, gives him a tongue-lashing so bitter that he goes out to drown himself. On the bank of the river, however, a clever thought suddenly comes to his mind; the work of his brain has not, after all, been entirely wasted. He decides upon a deal that will net him $10,000. Billy Higgins, a vaudeville student of several years, gave a pleasing interpretation of the role he was called upon to fill.

"At Home Abroad," a piece by Howard Dietz and Arthur Schwartz, had its premiere, September 19, 1935, in New York City. In constructing this review of two acts, the authors produced a travelogue, which was highly imaginative. Ethel Waters, the leading Negro actress, made the Hottentot, Potentate, and Steam Boat songs written for her by the authors stand out as the chief features of the production. Cast in a lovely costume, with golden bands, Ethel Waters appeared in a glittering jungle scene. After a month's run in New York, "At Home Abroad" played to appreciative audiences in Boston for two weeks. The play did much to introduce to the public a great actress, Ethel Waters.

OTHER WHITE PLAYWRIGHTS

Unfortunately, "Brown Sugar," by Bernie Angus, the colored Broadway production of November, 1937, was hardly considered a success. The Negro character does not ring true. Perhaps audiences and critics had become bored with the sordid life of the Negro "underworld." Then, too, the play was disjointed, and poorly acted. Accordingly, "Brown Sugar" ran for only a week. It is hardly a good play.

"Green Pastures," a widely known play, beginning in 1929, had an unusually long run on Broadway, three years to be exact. After that time, it took to the road and toured the United States and Canada. Richard B. Harrison, the character who played the role of the Lord in Marcus Connelly's "Green Pastures," was drawn toward drama as a profession by his mother who frequently took young Richard to the theatre in Detroit, Michigan, and in London, Canada, where he spent most of his youth. In Detroit, Harrison met Edward Weitz, who further encouraged his dramatic talent.

While playing in "Green Pastures" he had occasion to make a speech at the 135th Street Branch of the Y.M.C.A., New York City, on which occasion he acquainted his audience with the most important happenings of his career. Among other things, he spoke of having been an earnest student of Paul Laurence Dunbar, and William Shakespeare. To piece out his own education, he attended school whenever and wherever he found opportunity to learn something about the art of interpretative reading.

In 1891, Harrison toured Canada and the United States on Chautauqua and Lyceum circuits, giving public readings in tents, churches, schools and theatres. His interpretation of Shylock in the "Merchant of Venice" placed him among the best interpreters of that role in his day. During the interim, however, the eking out of a precarious existence forced him to do many odd jobs, such as waiting table and hopping bells. During the succeeding seven years, that is, from 1922 through 1929, he taught speech and drama at the Agricultural and Technical College, Greensboro, North Carolina. Writing of himself just before he died in 1935, Harrison said that he had never had as much as $500.00 at one time in his life.

Thinking that it might be sacrilegious for him to play the part of the Lord, he went to the outstanding ministers of New York City to get their reaction as to his playing the role in "The Green Pastures" before agreeing to take the part. They assured him that, rather than doing anything impious or sacrilegious, he would carry the part admirably. It was not, however, until after Mr. Connelly had had several conferences with him, that he finally agreed to sign with the company.

For his portrayal of the role of the Lord during the preceding year, the President of Boston University presented him with a Sigma key which no other actor, and no other Negro, had ever received.

So popular was the stage success "Green Pastures" that it was subsequently made into a moving picture, featuring Rex Ingram as the Lord, and Frank Wilson as Moses in the screen version. Seldom in the history of the stage has anything been so appealingly dramatic as the appearance of "De Lawd," when Gabriel cries out, "Gangway! Gangway! for the Lawd Gawd Jehovah." The scene was so touching and effective that not a sound came from the vast audience. With this reaction on the part of the audience Marcus Connelly and the sponsors had triumphed.

In the words of Connelly, "It is an attempt on the part of the author to present certain aspects of a living religion in terms of its believers."[12] The late Richard B. Harrison, hero and Lawd of the production, writing for the *Christian Herald* stated that "the play has been received as a portrayal of various Biblical events as they might be imagined by thousands of untutored Negroes of the deep South. These unlettered but devout black Christians think of Heaven as an eternal holiday, where elaborate fish-frys are plentiful, and where the Lord keeps a box of thunderbolts ready for the wicked of the earth."[13]

In this story, the incidents of the Bible have been adapted to the actual life and simple experiences of the Negro. Curiously enough, the most ludicrous point of the play is the fish-fry, but as James Weldon Johnson emphasizes, fish is far more agreeable and delicious as an everlastingly continuous diet than milk and honey.

As the curtain rises on the first scene, the audience observes Sunday School in session with a group of colored children bewildered and astounded as the uneducated minister places his personal interpretation on the Book of Genesis: "An' all de days of Methuselah were nine hund'ed an' sixty an' nine an' he died." Then after telling the little flock of other Biblical characters that lived to a ripe old age, he reminds them that he will preach from Noah, Sunday. Becoming befuddled when the children corner him on certain pertinent phases of the Book, Dishee evades their ques-

[12] "Just Like a Natchel Man," as quoted by R. B. Harrison, et al., *Christian Herald*, March, 1935, pp. 12-13, p. 44, p. 47.

[13] Harrison, *op. cit.*, p. 13.

tions with, "De answer is dat de Book ain't got time to go into all de details." However, he is certain that "De Lawd creates Adam and Eve, drives Cain clean out of de country, reproved his chillun for breaking the Sabbath with jazz music and crap games." "Green Pastures" is one of the best plays ever dramatized.

On June 7, 1932, James K. Millen's "Never No More" enjoyed a cordial premiere at the Hudson Theatre, New York City. The audience cringed, however, when the second act unfolded a heinous, lynching scene on the stage. Few details are omitted as the author reveals the wicked lynchers, the atrocious pyre-builders and the pitiful victim. Apparent flames penetrate the windows. Shrill crying is heard from the Negro as the depraved villains go about their task of American justice. Brothers, sisters and mother cry and beseech God to save their relative from the scoundrels, who are having what is often referred to as a Roman holiday. Those who witnessed the show were greatly moved by the grimmest of realities. Even seasoned critics said, "Never No More" did they want to see such a ghastly performance.

"Never No More" is simply the transmission to the stage of a southern inferno, in which Negroes are tortured. Gently leading up to his main business, Millen begins with a small group of innocent farmers, who are happy over their bountiful crop. Solomon, the black sheep, throws the family into pandemonium when he comes home and admits that he has killed a white girl. Instantly, vicinity-wide search gets under way, tracking the Negro to the shanty of his pious family, whose earnest petitions are insufficient to shunt a band of savages. This lack of friction and

94

conflict is the principal defect in an otherwise fair dramatization. Nevertheless, the escapade goes further toward stripping southern democracy of its glamor than anything since Walter White's *Fire in the Flint*. It is the kind of spectacle that causes the German people to snicker up their sleeves when they are reminded of their Jewish oppression by American politicians. It was a well dramatized performance, but these actual happenings bouncing back to white doorsteps could not be displayed even on liberal Broadway.

Rose McClendon, who holds a unique record in the annals of the American stage, assisted the author by being in the principal role of Mammy. Having been familiar with the ways of certain white folk, she easily and effectively submerged herself into the character of Mammy. The harassed and besieged brothers were well portrayed by Maurice McKinney and William L. Anderson. Leigh Whipper as the neighbor and Lew Payton as the deacon were particularly good.

In "Mamba's Daughter" was depicted the life and experiences of the huge, dull-witted Hagar with her picturesqueness, pathos, dialect and dry humor—set against a background of three centuries of Negro life in America. Du Bose and Dorothy Heyward made their drama all the more powerful by relating the miserable story of Hagar's devotion to her daughter, Liza.

Ethel Waters starred in the role of Hagar. For her support Guthrie McClintic selected splendid talent in the persons of Willie Bryant, the villain, Freda Washington as her daughter, and Georgette Harvey as her mother, Mamba.

In dramatizing their novel, "Mamba's Daughter,"

the Heywards have not written a play second to
"Porgy." In fact, it is a downright weak characterization of Negro life. Mother love, with its stereotyped
sacrifice, is hardly worth commending. Mamba and
Hagar taken as a composite of thousands of the deep
South have never been blessed with any wedding ceremony, and added to this tragedy is the fact that the
paternity of Hagar's child is unknown. And yet they
have an indomitable desire to protect the girl from
the sorrows they have experienced. No need or request of the child is too great. With self-denial and
sacrifice they insure her many cultural advantages de-
nied the average child. To the mother and grand-
mother it is consoling to observe that the girl reacts
favorably to music, art and training.

Despite the fact that "Mamba's Daughter" is a
dull, rambling story, Ethel Waters put vigor and life
into the piece without much aid from the lines. Time
and time again she saved the Heywards from floundering in their own folly. Her rich Negro diction
and natural pantomime were so eloquent that she
easily endeared her audience to her warmth and sweet-
ness. In a similar vein John Mason Brown of the
New York *Post* observed, "As a legitimate actress,
Miss Waters proves herself to be an exceptional performer. She is the perfect Hagar, if only the right
play had been written for her Hagar." Du Bose Heyward recognized the dramatic merit of Miss Waters
when he wrote, "We have come to know her, the play
has been written with her constantly in mind, it has
been produced, and she has received the acclaim that
she deserves."

Noting the disjointed and obvious faults of the
dramatization, Richard Lockridge of the New York

Sun said, "However, no play can be worthless in which an actress gives a profoundly stirring performance."

"Savage Rhythm," a drama by Harry Hamilton and Norman Foster, attempts to burlesque the Mississippi Negro's belief in sorcery. If the note in their preface may be trusted, the playwrights spent much time in the southern locality studying superstition and magic rites. Be that as it may, the piece approaches the lives of many Negroes. One of the conjur'-woman's granddaughters refuses to quit chasing men after bearing two illegitimate children. Another granddaughter is slain by the wife of the community dude. The fact that these Negroes consult the spirits instead of the law when punishment is to be meted out is the basis of the story. Instead of accusing the actual slayer the spirits point the finger of suspicion at the dude, who is indirectly responsible for the crime. When the spirits prevent his gun's firing at his tormentors, the neighbors chase him into the demon-infested swamps. This piece of trite dialogue was presented at the John Golden Theatre in February, 1931.

Though the play has no merit, at least sociologically, it did bring to the fore Venzuela Jones and Vivian Blake. Their appearance was almost as picturesque as that of Juano Hernandez, who played the rustic lover, and Ernest R. Whitman, who played the sheik.

"Singing the Blues," written and produced in 1931 by John McGowan, appeared with its set of scenes in Harlem's "hot spots." Although cabaret activity abounds, the play has characterization, suspense, theme and plot.

The scene of action shifts from Chicago to New York. Committing murder in Chicago, the villain flees East to be embraced by a beautiful night club singer, heroine of the play and actress in Crocker's cabaret. She is also the sweetheart of Crocker, who swears revenge and helps the detectives in their pursuit of the murderer. Only a subtle move on the part of the girl prevents officers' bullets from destroying the crapshooting slayer of Chicago.

The material is not original; yet the play is refreshing. When it was produced in New York, Frank Wilson played the role of Crocker. Isabelle Washington was in the leading feminine role, and Jack Carter as usual made a good villain.

Lew Leslie's rhapsodic review of Harlem's bourgeois talent, "Black Birds of 1939," was successfully presented in the Hudson Theatre, New York City, in February, 1939. Sepia talent of first rank seems to have been busy in "Hot Mikado," for the names of no stars were mentioned on the program. Brooks Atkinson, who reviewed the conglomeration for the New York *Times,* stated, "Lew Leslie, who has been blackbirding for twelve years never changes his formula. . . . . Noise to him is the genius of Negro entertainment. There are no top flight performers or rare setting. The sketches are routine and heavy handed. Little more than exhaustion comes out of the colored carnival."

In addition to Rosamond Johnson's choir, which delightfully entertained the audience with its singing of "Rhapsody in Blue," the radiant Lena Horne was rated sensational in her singing of "Thursday" and "You Are So Indifferent." Hamtree Harrington, Dewey Markam, Tim Moore and Joe Byrd with their jests and antics were indeed amusing. It is said, too, that the dancing was not to be sniffed at, for this scene was compared to a jungle holiday, when the feet of Ralph Brown and others in the cast thrilled the audience with their ecstatic capers. If the audiences gathered to see frolicsome leaps and springing, tap dancing, skipping and cataleptic trances done by rapturous fools, they did not regret the price of their ticket.

Born in 1885 out of chaos and temperament, and paraded on a wave of facetious episodes, the original "Mikado" of Gilbert and Sullivan has at last been peopled with an all-Negro cast and set to modernized rhythm by Michael Todd.[1] In 1934, Todd rearranged the "Mikado," inserted provision for a number of chorus girls, together with modern popular features, and pronounced his craftsmanship "The Hot Mikado." The press has referred to it as the most lavished extravaganza since the burlesque days of Ziegfeld. From the time the curtain rises until the final tapping of Bill Robinson, the show is as breezy and thrilling a play as Broadway has seen in many a day; in fact, thinks William Doll, as the American theatre has ever seen. The melody, acrobats, swing, jazz, singing and "hot" dancing are so gay and gorgeous that they are symphonic. This funny show has a cast which made Broadway merry before leaving the Bradhurst Theatre for the Music Hall at the 1939 World's Fair.

The Broadway version has been greatly changed and concentrated by Hassard Short, packing two hours of entertainment into one. In his redirecting, he has neatly added several more jitterbugs, whose dancing and interpretation of "Three Little Maids from School" and "The Flowers That Bloom in the Spring" look and sound as if Cab Calloway and Jimmie Lunceford were in the Cotton Club at the same time.

[1] See program of "Hot Mikado," World's Fair Music Hall, 1939.

THE NEGRO AND THE DRAMA

The excellent costumes are fantastic to the nth degree, especially that of Maurice Ellis. As Pooh-Bah he declares that he "can trace his ancestors back to a 'protospasmal' globule." In addition, he says that he will accept the posts of the high officers of State, who are too proud to serve under an ex-house painter. His inclusion of the Minister of Propaganda and Enlightenment would suggest that he is mildly satirizing Herr Hitler.

In "Hot Mikado," Robert Parrish (Nanki Poo) made his first Broadway bow. Discovered by Major Bowes' radio programs on which he was a successful contestant, he has climbed rapidly in the last two of his twenty-four years. His radio solo of "That's Why Darkies Were Born" accelerated his ascension, and resulted in a prolonged engagement in Australia, where his popularity was of such that he was offered a return engagement. Meanwhile, his American radio and recording offers have been so prevalent that the officials of "Hot Mikado" considered themselves fortunate in retaining him in their company.

Freddie Robinson (Nanki-Poo) has been a very busy actor in and around Broadway ever since he left his small town where he was a blacksmith. Beginning as a trumpet-player in "Broadway Rastus," he immediately became a star of the production. Many theatre-goers have not forgot his interpretation of "Onions" in "Shuffle Along." Added to these feats, he has played in "Chocolate Dandies," "Brown Buddies," and Calloway's "Hi De Ho."

Alice Harris (Yum-Yum) of Boston was discovered as a musical student in Chicago where she began her dramatic career. Featured as a star in "Going to Town," she has also toured as a brilliant entertainer with the band of Noble Sissle, and has sung with Buck and Bubbles.

J. A. Lillard (Pish Tush), whose tenor voice has been compared to Caruso's, has appeared in Russian, Italian and Hebrew concerts. As first tenor in "Showboat," he moved on to play in "Brown Buddies," "Black Birds," "Virginia" and has crowned his achievements with the portrayal of an attorney in "Sing Out the News."

Frances Brock (Pitti-Sing) started as a chorister, becoming soon a soloist in Juano Hernandez' male group. Three of her musical comedies have been produced by amateurs. The night clubs of New York have received her warmly. Harlem theatres have acclaimed her singing.

Rosetta Lee Noire (Peep Bo) has written considerable and sung over the air. She has been seen in "Run Little Chillun," "Eastern Star," "Bassa Moona," "The Blue Bird," and "Porgy."

Needless to say, Bill Robinson is the great star of this gleaming "Hot Mikado," given as a preview on June 20, 1939, for the World's Fair employees, who rocked the Hall of Music with enthusiasm as he "turned on the steam" with his pattering feet. Thus, with a cast of this sort, it is not difficult to understand that though the thread of the story is weak, it was a good show both on Broadway and at the World's Fair.

Abigail (Abbie) Mitchell made her Broadway debut in 1910 with Williams and Walker in "Bandanna Land." In 1933 she played Binnie in "Stevedore," and subsequently Cora in "Mulatto." The production in which she plays second only to the main character is "The Little Foxes," featuring Tallulah Bankhead, currently showing at the National Theatre, off Broadway. Her stage business, movement, and scintillating humor so sparkle that she is agreeably welcomed on each of her appearances.

Playing a delightful role also in "The Little Foxes" is John Marriot, who, as Cal, operated an elevator in "Three Men on a Horse." He was the sullen prisoner in "Chalked Out," and virtually made the cracking of a whip, with its sharp sound and resonant blows, speak the will of an overseer as Simon Legree's slave-driver in George Abbot's "Sweet River."

The man whose endless chain of small roles probably outnumber all others is Leigh Whipper. In mixed features he is best known for his role in "Stevedore." However, when "Of Mice and Men" was a Broadway hit, he had an important role, and now that the production is being converted into a moving picture, he is being cast in his original role. Together with Richard Huey and Jean Henderson he had an entertaining role in "Three Men on a Horse."

A ranking actress of stage, radio, and screen is Gee Gee James. Miss James made her first stage appearance in a Negro stock company in Philadelphia, her birthplace. When but a young girl, she went to New York to play as a chorine. The producer of "Hot Rhythm" noted her rich, musical sounds and forthwith had her to sing several numbers that greatly aided in putting the play "across the footlights." The notice she received in "Hot Rhythm" was brought to the attention of Cab and Blanche Calloway, Jimmie Lunceford, Don Redman, Chick Webb and orchestras of others with whom she has played. Such luminaries as Kate Smith, Rudy Vallee and Ruth Chatterton have made use of her talent in their broadcasts. She was one of the stars in Fleischmann's Yeast all-colored show over the air. She also played a criminal role in the "Gibson Family" over the air. Fame came to her as "Aunt Jemima" in Thomas Riggs' "Quaker Party." Broadway gave her a chance for the first time in the season of 1938 in "Michael Drops In." Her portrayal of Clementine in "No Time for Comedy," currently playing, has done much to enhance her ascendancy in public favor. In this production she is not a ludicrous servant, but delights the audience with her frivolity almost as much as Katherine Cornell, the leading character, does with hers.

In other productions have appeared and are appearing Oscar Pope, John Merriott, and Frances Williams in "You Can't Take It With You"; Eddie Green and Richard Huey in "I Must Love Some One"; Georgette Harvey, Lou Payton and Richard Huey in "Solid South"; Georgette Harvey in "Behind the Red Lights"; Marietta Canty and Frank Wilson in "Kiss the Boys Goodbye"; Eula Bell Moore in "Brother Rat"; Hubert Brown and Emory Richardson in "Abe Lincoln in Illinois"; a Negro quartette in "Hell's a Poppin"; Oscar Polk and Hattie McDaniels in "Gone with the Wind." Arthur Arent, who wrote "One Third of a Nation," included in the play scenes and characters of Harlem life. Alexander Lovejoy has been in Hollywood with Metro-Goldwyn-Mayer for five years. Eddie Rochester has played delightfully with Jack Benny in "Man About Town."

DRAMA OF MIXED CASTS

At the present time there is rapidly evolving the type of drama that requires a mixed cast. Many of the social and humanitarian plays of the past decades have had one or two persons of the opposite race play a small role. But in such a cast in which the star is a Negro, there is a situation of unusual interest. The drama, "As Thousands Cheer," presented during May, June, July, and August, 1934, and starring Ethel Waters, was so popularly received that seats were reserved six weeks in advance. This satirical revue by Irvin Berlin and Moss Hart was a satisfying bit of entertainment.

Dramatic critics momentarily forgot that anybody except Ethel Waters was of importance to the production. She was referred to as a name that makes news; a personality that did her role excellently, and marvelously. Others said she was exhilarating. Though she had introduced 50 song hits to Broadway, the singing of her three favorites: "Heat Waves," "Stormy Weather," "Dinah," and a brilliant impersonation of Josephine Baker's pining for Harlem in Paris furnished the audience with a gaiety that was light and charming.[14] Her soothing interpretation of "Am I Blue" added zest and pleasure to "On with the Show."

At thirty-nine, Ethel Waters proved that she is a legitimate actress of exceptional talent. Ethel was born in the slums of Chester, Pennsylvania, to a thirteen-year-old mother who washed clothes for the scum of a nearby railroad. At eleven she, too, was a washgirl. At thirteen, she was a bride. At seventeen, she was discovered in a cabaret at a table with a group of friends. Two men who heard her sing, arranged for her to go to Baltimore to appear in the Lincoln Theatre. For nine dollars a week, she soothed the audience with W. C. Handy's "St. Louis Blues."

[14] The New York *Post*, May 6, 1930.

From then on, she rose rapidly in popular favor. Cabaret parties enjoyed her singing. Negro orchestras featured her. She toured the West and South. Musical companies and stock shows considered themselves fortunate when she toured with them "to help put the show over." She was a favorite at the Cotton Club, Small's Paradise, and Connie's Inn. Broadway heard of her, and had her in its shows. Fame came to her in 1934 when she starred in "As Thousands Cheer." In that year she earned $76,000.

Ethel Waters' great dramatic triumph came to her when she received the leading role in Du Bose and Dorothy Heyward's "Mamba's Daughter." Heyward says that they did not see her on the screen in "On With the Show." Mrs. Heyward, however, saw her on Broadway in Lew Leslie's "Rhapsody in Black." Mrs. Heyward felt that after ten years of patience she had at last seen the actress who could play Hagar. The Heywards decided forthwith that whoever produced the play would, by agreement, use Ethel Waters in the role of Hagar.

By arrangement or chance, the Heywards and Ethel met at a reception. Before many minutes had lapsed, Mrs. Heyward and Ethel Waters had begun to converse. The latter astonished the author of the novel by saying, "I have read a novel named 'Mamba's Daughter.' There is a character in there, Hagar, that I'd like to play." Then, as reported by Du Bose Heyward in the *Theatre Arts Monthly,* Mrs. Heyward related to her the ambitions of the Heywards to dramatize the play with her in the main role. Soon after this conversation, it appeared that the Heywards' plans would be frustrated because of the fascinating offers Ethel received to appear in Broadway musical comedies. But the actress reminded them that nothing would alter her determination to play Hagar. And as John Mason Brown puts it, she not only played the role, but helped to write it, as she so artistically unfolded the story. Her eloquent diction and pantomime helped her to turn it into a stage performance even when it appeared as if it were written for a silent moving picture. On his second visit to see the show, January 14, 1939, Brooks Atkinson wrote:

"It is perfectly plain that Miss Waters is giving a valiant performance in a play that may be clumsily put together. For a number of years Miss Waters has had a prominent niche in the Hall of Fame reserved for the great music-hall singers; give her at any time a gusty song, and she could melt a frigid audience into complete malleability. Now, in her first dramatic role, she proves that she can carry over into a play that same power of reducing an audience to a state of fervent admiration."

HARLEM NEGRO ACTORS PERFORM IN CANADA

Richard Huey, product of Louisiana and Hampton Institute, who upon coming to New York in 1923, did small roles and subsequently larger ones, was instrumental in taking a group of colored players to Canada to produce "Porgy" and "In Abraham's Bosom." While in Canada, he and his troupe also produced "Harlem," the theme of which dealt with Negro life and character of New York.

Saturday, November 5, 1932, The Toronto *Evening Telegram* carried these headlines:

Pulitzer Play at the Empire.
Tragedy Well Portrayed in "In Abraham's Bosom."

OTHER WHITE PLAYWRIGHTS

The same issue of The *Telegram* also stated, "Not often have Toronto play-goers seen a poignant tragedy more completely acted than 'In Abraham's Bosom' presented at the Empire by a Negro cast. It is not a tragedy that will be performed often, because without Negro actors, it would be lifeless. Thomas Mosely who took the role in the original play and played the part of 'Porgy' earlier this season is an unusually fine actor."[15]

SUMMARY

In 1909, Edward Sheldon focused attention upon the Negro from an angle somewhat different from any attempt since the Civil War. He went to the core of the race problem and dramatized it in his "The Nigger." He was followed by Ridgley Torrence's three one-act plays. With the Negro as thematic material, Eugene O'Neill wrote seven plays, from 1918 to 1924, dealing with the Negro. Paul Green made a specialty of dramatizing Negro themes. Coming to the front in 1920, with his "In Abraham's Bosom,"[16] he consistently dealt with Negro material. Other such writers deserving of consideration are David Belasco, Du Bose and Dorothy Heyward, Lew Leslie, John Wexley, George Sklar, Paul Peters, and Marcus Cook Connelly. They have brought to the fore, a subject hitherto hardly touched. It was the efforts of these playwrights who, by their treatment of the Negro as thematic material enabled the Negro to come before the public in serious drama.

[15] *The Evening Telegram*, November 5, 1932.
[16] James W. Johnson, *Black Manhattan*. New York: Alfred Knopf, 1930, pp. 130-135.

CHAPTER VII

RECENT DRAMA OF NEGRO AUTHORSHIP

Since the Great War, a number of Negro dramatists have attained national reputation. While the white authors have concerned themselves with the commercial aspect of Negro material, the Negro dramatist has been imbued with a determination to present the realistic phase of Negro life, which has heretofore been neglected. The Negro dramatist has been interested in the subject of Negro drama from the point of view of oppression, exploitation, humiliation, illegitimacy, folklore, and natural mimicry.

The reasons for a dearth of Negro dramatic productions have been various. Randolph Edmonds, professor of dramatics at Dillard University, advances one of several arguments when he suggests that plays of Negro authorship have been crippled by too much and too prolonged haranguing.[1] The dramatic editor of the Chicago *Defender* is of the opinion that selfish motivations have been responsible, in that Negro authors have concerned themselves too much with themes concerning racial friction, oppression, exploitation, and consorting of white men with colored women.[2] The financial aspect of production has also tended to discourage Negro authorship. Only the rare few have been willing to go to the expense of staging a show without previous guarantee of financial success. The

[1] Randolph Edmonds, ''Some Reflections on the Theatre,'' *Opportunity*, October, 1930, pp. 303-335.
[2] *Chicago Defender*, May 3, 1930.

playwrights themselves have not been able to finance the venture. Hence, their scripts have not come before the public.

In 1920, Frank Wilson, a postal clerk, wrote his "Sugar Cane." This drama, while it was not pretentious, was superior to many of the plays written during the period. Wilson laid the scene of "Sugar Cane" in a modest home of contemporary Georgia. The circumstances surrounding the story deal with Paul, his wife, and their daughter, the last of whose actions create in the parents a bit of unpleasant suspicion. Within a period of three months, they become definitely aware of the fact that their daughter, Martha, has been violated. Martha names a young colored man, Howard Hill, who stayed with the family when he was home from the North on a short visit.

All hearts go out in sympathy for Martha when she, in a sense of shame and remorse, leaves home. Meanwhile, Fred, a son, voices certain suspicions to his parents concerning the movements of Lee Drayton, a white man who lives near by. Despite the fact that still further gossip had reached his ears, the father has such implicit confidence in white people that he does not, for a second, suppose that Lee Drayton, of all people, would seduce his daughter, and what is more he does not take kindly to Fred's accusation. Notwithstanding the fact that the finger of suspicion unmistakably points to the white man, the father swears vengeance against Howard Hill, declaring that he will kill the colored youth on sight. That, however, Martha's father fails to do, because she soon bears the child. Its appearance shows that it is, in reality, the child of a white man.

In 1928, Frank Wilson, who was also starring at the

time in "Porgy," actually captivated Broadway audiences with his "Meek Mose" which had its premiere at the Princess Theatre, January 23, 1928.

Docile Mose is supposed to be a patriarch among the better colored citizens of a Texas community. On the other hand, among the lower class he is referred to as a "church nigger of the white folks type," who relies upon the strength derived from Biblical quotations for his economic and social salvation. "Blessed are the meek, for they shall inherit the earth," Mose reminds the neighbors, one of whom disdainfully tells him that "he is full of rabbits." The whites admit that he is partly right, in that the Mighty Meek will inherit the earth. When the landlords evict him and his companions from the shacks, he advises his followers that the Lord will provide. Toward the end of the piece when disease and famine befall them, the group attempt to murder their leader because he appears to be a false prophet. As conditions become worse for old Mose, and the scripture fails to support him, oil is suddenly discovered on his land; whereupon, the entire community rejoices with spirituals, which furnish the production with its most satisfying bit of relief.

Wilson's characterization of the cynical wife of the hero has been considered by critics as perfect craftsmanship. She never wavered from the part assigned to her by the playwright. For the creation of her role and her husband's, alone, Frank Wilson deserves much credit. He has done a creditable piece of work.

During the year 1921, a young government clerk, Willis Richardson, had the dream of his ambition realized with the production "The Deacon's Awakening," at St. Paul, Minnesota. In May, 1923, he enjoyed the distinction of having his "The Chip Woman's Fortune," produced, along with Oscar Wilde's "Salome," by the Ethiopian Art Players of New York. The Ethiopian Art Players, sponsored by Sherwood Anderson and Raymond O'Neill, showed another advancement realized by dramatic minded Negroes. No less important is the fact that Richardson's play was honored by them. In 1923, also, the Howard University Players produced his "Mortgaged." In 1925, he was awarded the Amy Spingarn Medal for having written "The Broken Banjo." This drama has an interesting plot, story and theme, and presents a sympathetic discussion of the native characteristics of Negro life. Technically, but interestingly woven, the play has all the characteristics of a good drama and depicts the carefree life of many a happy-go-lucky parasite who lives on the earnings of his relatives. It is small wonder that the musically minded husband gets tired of supporting the shiftless relative, who dawdles around the house day in and day out. And it is the last straw when the easy-going kinsman not only breaks the husband's banjo, but turns the husband over to the police on a false accusation of murder.

Upon the completion of that piece, Mr. Richardson turned editor, and compiled a collection of plays entitled *Plays and Pageants from the Life of the Negro.* In 1935, he collaborated with Mary Miller in *Negro History in Thirteen Plays.* It was Mr. Richardson's opinion, expressed in the preface of that work, that his sponsors were interested in a collection of drama without dialect, with a Negro theme, and written by Negroes.[3] The motive was to satisfy school children

[3] W. Richardson, *Plays and Pageants from the Life of the Negro.* The Associated Publishers, Washington, D. C., 1935, p. 11.

who were interested in Negro drama.

Some of these plays are of Mr. Richardson's own authorship, possessing a comparatively fair dramatic technique. The prolonged classical speeches interspersed in the plays may be one reason for their lack of great merit. One play had its setting in the period just before Christ; another had its theme in the future, far beyond the present time. Few dramatists have reached that stage of their development at which critics and lay audiences would give more than a passing notice to their interpretation of life before Christ, or even a "King's Dilemma" that has its setting in some distant future. The "House of Sham" which is more timely, and comes nearer to vital, present-day experiences touches somewhat upon morals. "Riding the Goat," a story dealing with secret organizations, has comic spots, but here again one wonders if a more substantial play would not have satisfied better the purpose of the sponsors. But when one thinks of the difficult task of the editor, one should perhaps be sparing of adverse criticism. Believing as he did that one of the best ways to learn history is to have it dramatized, Richardson has done a commendable job in portraying the role that the Negro has played in the development of civilization.

John Matheus' "Ti Yette," one of the collection, which has its setting in New Orleans, in 1855, again shows the Negro author's concern over the virtue of Negro women. The ire of Racine is raised to deadly pitch on learning that old man Rhubotham, a white lawyer, has fallen in love with his sister. Heartbroken, he becomes desperate when his sister pays no heed to his admonition that such men as Rhubotham, who proposes to marry her, are seducers of women and betrayers of liberty. But the charming creole has no desire to solve racial problems, for "what difference does it make so long as we are both in love?" Misfortune begins its visitations upon Racine in earnest when, in addition to losing his appetite because his sister "bites me with moral passion and poison," the white lawyer has the couple haled before the court on the accusation that they are not brother and sister. Amateurs throughout the South and West have enjoyed giving "Ti Yette," for it is full of truth and entertainment, and is fairly well written.

With a sincere purpose, Dennis Donoghue in October, 1933, attempted to rationalize the Scottsboro, Alabama, case in "Legal Murder." Unlike John Wexley, however, who used the same material for his "They Shall Not Die," Donoghue failed of his goal. Without question, the indictment which the piece makes against the Scottsboro officials is true and just, but the material is handled in such a way as to produce a bungled effect. When the playwright lacks authentic information, he resorts to his imagination. The author shows some degree of dramatic technique in the trial scene, when the piece arrives at the crucial point. This scene which is a reproduction of the original trial is effectively done, and forces one to cringe as he witnesses how inhumane a court and jury can be.

Of the characters, the New York lawyer is by far, the most superior. There is a distinct contrast between him and his southern opponent. The defendants carry out their roles with credit, singing spirituals when their difficulties increase. Perhaps the play would have run longer than three nights had it not (it is said) been for the fact that the Theatre Guild bought out the play for $800.00.

THE NEGRO AND THE DRAMA

Even though he is an inexperienced dramatist, Dennis Donoghue is to be commended on his sincerity of purpose. Becoming irritated with some of the practices and customs of American life, he desires to express himself in this form of literature. As is true of many Negro authors, he shows in his play his disgust and anger with social oppression. It compares favorably with "They Shall Not Die," which is a good play.

Music rather than drama of Negro authorship enjoyed unprecedented favor in 1933, with the production of Hall Johnson's "Run Little Chillun." This fantasy, which approached its one hundredth performance, acquired its public interest by the fact that it was steeped in spirituals. The play was more than a group of spirituals dramatized. The author says "It is the passionate outcry of a race, and the poetic expression of the Negro mind."[4]

Commenting on the play when it was produced in 1933, The New York Herald *Tribune* observed, "That Negro fantasy . . . is something between, and something of all of them—melodrama in the real and true sense of the word."[5] Despite its faults, and the fact that spirituals were its greatest assets, the play added one further proof that the Negro could write drama.

"Mulatto" by the poet, Langston Hughes, which was presented continuously until December 9, 1937, was first put on at the Vanderbilt Theatre, October 24, 1935. The story attempts to narrate the tragic confusion of the people whose blood is half white, half black. Hughes has aimed to paint the social status of such a class, and has chosen Georgia for his locale. One of the best features of the play is the evidence

[4] Anonymous, Amsterdam *News*, November 28, 1933.
[5] New York *Herald Tribune*, August 12, 1933.

it gives of the apparent earnestness of the young dramatist's purpose. Without question, as his poetry and novels also indicate, he has written about a theme that has given him great concern.

Colonel Norwood, a southern gentleman, is taken as a type of the millions of his like in the South, while Cora Lewis, his colored housekeeper and mistress, is the mother of his mulattoes, and "the woman in the case." The status of the mulatto children, at present, creates no great social problem, even though the white American father refuses to recognize the illegitimate children. Driven to their mother's group, they lose their rightful heritage.

> My old man died in a fine big house
> My ma died in a shack
> I wonder where I'm gonna die,
> Being neither white nor black.

Hughes' play inspires sympathy in the northern white woman for her southern sister's predicament since the latter, as a wife, has to compete against a woman of another race, inferior in social background and breeding. The author also inspires the colored woman who sees in her white husband a champion of her civil and social rights. Many of both groups assert that any woman who is good enough to bear children for a man, is good enough to be recognized publicly with him and their children.

Resentment is also engendered in both groups when Colonel Norwood refuses, time and again, to recognize Robert Lewis, his son, as his own flesh and blood. Likewise, they resent his attitude toward Sally Lewis, Robert's sister, who typifies thousands of other mulatto girls. She is forced to submit to indignities;

in fact, she is obliged to stoop to the level of a hired harlot, and roam about in the kitchen, although she is in her own father's house. The first suspense for the audience takes place near the end of the first act when Billie Norwood comes home from college, and desires to act as any other person would under the circumstances. When he asserts that he is a human being, there is serious conflict in the home. Here is youth against age, black against white, the old social system against the new. But the Colonel would have none of this! It is against his custom, his social system, his caste and code. He is white—his son black. So bitterly does he resent his son's intrusion into his front door, that he draws a gun, and in the scuffle is killed.

Talbot, overseer of Norwood's plantation, has a dramatic scene with Robert at the beginning of the second act. This villain of the play draws a gun on the colored son who is a servant in his own father's house, and tries to force a confession that the son killed the father. Here is suspense again, but nothing serious happens as the scene ends in contentious dialogue.

Another suspense occurs when Sally is being fondled by the villain, who says, "Black women are only good for two things—to beat and to love." When he clutches her in his arms, she struggles. Yet during the entire incident Cora, the mother, is in the kitchen, and apparently hears not a word.

Hughes again indicates dramatic ability in the scene in which he builds up a splendid climax at the end of the second act, when Cora voices her feelings over the body of her dead mate. Her monologue is a masterpiece, and a fitting climax.

Hughes should be given credit for the frame-work of his play, despite the fact that Brooks Atkinson of the New York *Times* accused him of artlessness.[6] The right words are used in the right place, and by the right characters. "Mulatto" drives home a fine point in the death of Bobbie, who is slain by a mob. Like the "Man without a Country" he was marked to die as a martyr for a cause.

The production, when presented in New York City, obviously had a mixed cast, with Mercedes Gilbert, who succeeded the late Rose McClendon, in the title-role. She received prolonged applause for her splendid characterization of the mother of Colonel Norwood's children. "Mulatto" is by far Hughes' best play to date.

Produced during the golden year of 1929 when bootlegged liquor was the beverage of the Harlem Negro, "Harlem" centers its attention on gin parties and whatever other vice this borough had to offer. After a short Broadway run which began February 20, 1929, the production moved over into Canada, under the direction of Richard Huey. When this sketch of Harlem life was presented in New York, Robert Littell, dramatic critic, observed that this melodramatic story seems truer and better than the majority of this season's offering. These aspects of Negro life and character were put together by Wallace Thurman (Negro), assisted by William Rapp.

Interest of the story lies in the fact that it is an actual reproduction of the average Negro's existence in New York City. These authors who knew their subjects thoroughly were acquainted with house rent-parties designed, on Saturday night, with the idea of meeting the rent agent Monday. Even the details of

[6] The New York *Times*, October 25, 1935.

charging admission, the bootlegging of liquor, the hiring of two or three cheap musicians and the selling of food are herein dramatized. The murder phase of the story is chocked full of clicks, trickery and clues as a North Carolina family finds itself tangled in the bewilderment of riotous life. Gunmen and gamblers, whose occupation is the collecting of pennies on digits of the clearing house statements attend the party. Intricate rackets embrace powerful bosses, runners and gun-toters; hence murder, seduction and framing enter the play.

Robert Littell, who is credited with knowing what constitutes good acting, felt that it was Isabelle Washington's performance which lifted the play out of the category of melodrama, whereas Brooks Atkinson of the New York *Times* was of the opinion that Inez Clough, the confused mother, lent dignity to the play, with the assistance of Frank Badham and Billy Andrews, the villains. These three at least helped a good show to be a better show.

Rudolph Fisher, better known as a novelist, if the "Walls of Jericho" is any evidence, presents in "Conjur Man Dies" a sociological, hocus pocus in this piece of sorcery. The conservative critic, Brooks Atkinson of the New York *Times* considered it verbose and amateurish, yet Harlem audiences were exhilarated and enlivened when it was produced at the Lafayette Theatre, beginning March 12, 1936.

Serious doings get underway in an undertaking parlor in which Frimbo, the conjure man, is apparently slain. Detectives begin sleuthing with the idea of catching the assassin, only to be astounded with the apparent resurrection of Frimbo. At this halfway point, Fisher displays a degree of dramaturgy, for he dextrously guides the police through perplexing problems; moreover, he causes the audience and reader to squirm as he heaps horror and terror upon superstition. Only the appearance of a regal black magician prevents the play being too weird.

Notwithstanding its box-office appeal, "Conjur Man" would waste much time and effort of an amateur group attempting to produce it, for the play has little intrinsic merit. With all its mediocrity and repetitious dialogue, the play had a short run by the Brattleboro Theatre, which presented it at the St. Felix Street Playhouse, Brooklyn, New York. With Pearl Gaines, Al Stokes, Laura Bowman, Morris McKinny, Robert Harvey, Juanita Hall, Robert Wilson and Clyde Turner, the Brattleboro Theatre had a fairly competent cast. Worse shows have been written and presented, and yet with Maurice McKinney portraying the ludicrous role of "Rev. Green" and the occasional lively moments of Pearl Gaines, the piece had a few thrilling spots. If the truth were asserted, the entire cast was more superior as actors than Miss Freeman was as playwright, for she has badly put together some inconsequential material.

MUSICAL COMEDY

The greatest evidence that there are and have been Negroes who can write appealing drama, with the elements of comedy that would arrest the attention of the theatrical public, appeared in 1921. In that year Miller and Lyles, assisted by Blake and Sissle, came out with that thrilling musical comedy, "Shuffle Along." When it played to audiences in the District of Columbia for two weeks, it gave a satisfaction that Washingtonians have not yet forgot. Press agents and theatre-goers hailed it as the best musical comedy that Washington had seen in many years. The snappy artistically-sung songs were a part of the production, in fact, an important part—songs such as "Bandana Days," "Gipsy Blues," "I'm Wild About Harry," and "Shuffle Along." The feature, however, that pleased the audiences most was the intriguing, subtle plot which was originated and constructed by F. E. Miller and Aubrey Lyles. Moreover, the latter had parts in the cast. The theme dealt with a business enterprise (grocery store), in which Miller and Lyles were engaged. The business thrived for a while, at least, until one of the black-faced comedians stole all of the money and left the city; whereupon a medley of inquiries by the players, half-sung, half-spoken, followed. The inquiries were:

"Everybody wants to know where the money is gone.
Everybody wants to know where the money is gone."

After leaving Washington where the troupe had made its debut, it went to Philadelphia, and thence to the Sixty-third Street Theatre, New York, where it took the city by storm. Among the critics who reviewed it, Alain Locke seems to have been the most appreciative of the merits of the comedy. Quoting Max Rinehardt, he wrote of the players, "They are highly original in spite of triteness, and artistic in spite of superficial crudeness." Reinhardt may have also discerned, together with other critics, that the production had freshness and vigor, with emotional responses, intensity of mood, and spontaneous stagecraft.

Miller and Lyles had assembled for this show a cast of dancers, singers and actors with uncommon aptitude. The company had such stars as the late Florence

Mills, Revella Hughes, Gertrude Saunders, and Lottie Gee, supported by a beautiful costumed chorus. After playing in New York houses for a year, the troupe enjoyed an eighteen month tour.

Before the interest in "Shuffle Along had hardly cooled, Miller and Lyles, who were by now the two best known Negro dramatists of the race, carried to Broadway another brisk, and thrilling production, "Running Wild." While this latter ambitious attempt was not to be classed with the former, perhaps its greatest feature was its introduction of the Charleston dance. Like most American dances, it was a distinct Negro creation, heretofore little known except in Harlem and its native South Carolina. But following its association with "Running Wild," it suddenly became not only nationally but internationally accepted.

SUMMARY

In the recent drama produced by the Negro, playwrights have made a step forward in portraying Negro life as it is. At the same time these authors have boldly resorted to propaganda in exposing the evils from which Negroes suffer. These writers have not solved the entire problem of dramaturgy which they face, probably for the reason that they have not given sufficient attention to the audience itself and have been unable to conceal more cleverly the purpose to change the public attitude toward the race. The Negro writers of musical comedy have shown signs of progress in drawing upon the Negroes' inherently comical nature.

CHAPTER VIII

THE LITTLE THEATRE MOVEMENT

Writing, in 1921, on the Negro in Drama, Montgomery Gregory, then professor of Dramatic Literature at Howard University, said:

"Howard University has undertaken a sincere movement to lay the foundation of the Negro theatre. It has established a department of dramatic art with Marie Moore Forest, nationally known as director of drama and pageantry, and Cleon Thorckmorton, the designer of the scenery for the 'Emperor Jones' and 'Spring' associated in its direction . . . The Howard Players have already won the commendation of the public and the dramatic critics by the excellence of their productions. The scenery and costumes are executed by the players in our work shop. In addition to other performances, they presented 'The Emperor Jones' with Charles Gilpin in the title-role at the Belasco Theatre in Washington, D. C., last year. Our work has the endorsement of such dramatic critics as Kenneth McGown of the *Theatre Arts Magazine,* Heywood Broun of the New York *World,* Eugene O'Neill, Ridgeley Torrence, and the Provincetown Players."[1]

Unfortunately, the movement somewhat declined at Howard University in the absence of Professor Gregory, who resigned his professorship soon after the Howard venture was started. However, it has been revived under Sterling Brown and Jas. W. Butcher. The seed of this idea has taken root and spread in the South and Southwest; little theatres and groups have

[1] Montgomery Gregory, "The Negro Actor," *The New Republic,* November 16, 1921, p. 350.

122

rapidly developed in these sections, and to some extent in the West. It is reported from as far away as the State of Washington that the little theatre is progressing there. Likewise, from Louisville, Kentucky, comes interesting news of its little theatre. The Gilpin Players of Cleveland, Ohio, are very enthusiastic over their organization and its productions. Moreover, colleges in recent years have manifested much interest in amateur productions, and the value they have in developing students. North Carolina for the past five years has had an annual dramatic tournament in which most of the liberal minded colleges of the State have participated. Considerable interest and enthusiasm have been manifested among the students.

Since 1930, the Morgan College Players have perhaps surpassed the efforts of most other colleges. The passage quoted below from the foreword in Randolph Edmonds' "Six Plays for a Negro Theatre," by Professor Frederick H. Enoch, teacher of drama, University of North Carolina, not only bears out the truth of this statement, but takes notice of the increasing interest that is now displayed in drama by Negro colleges. "There is today a dramatic awakening among the young people of our Negro colleges and universities in the South toward a theatre and drama of their own people. Foremost, perhaps, in this new movement is Randolph Edmonds, teacher of English and dramatic director in Morgan College, Baltimore. Last spring when I served as critic judge in the third annual tournament of the Negro Inter-Collegiate Dramatic Association in Richmond, I saw an exciting performance of Mr. Edmonds' folk-play of sawmill life. In 'Bad Men' I was much impressed with the enthusiasm, the freshness, and the imagination of the young playwright's work."[2]

In the preface to the same volume, Edmonds very timely states, "This volume of plays is intended primarily for use in the Negro Little Theatre, where there has been for many years a great need for plays of Negro life written by Negroes. It is hoped, of course, that they will find their way into the repertory of other groups as well; for, if plays are really worthwhile, they ought to contain some universal elements that will rise above the narrow confines of the nation or race of the cast of characters.

"I am fully aware of the fact that there are many Negroes who do not like dialect plays. It has long been my opinion, however, that it is not the crude expressions of the peasant characters that contribute to this dislike; but rather the repelling atmosphere and the psychology of the inferior that somehow creep into the peasant plays of the most unbiased authors of other racial groups."[3]

Those who would question the genuine merit of folk-plays might be brought to a more exact realization of that merit by the following quotation:

"These plays have worthwhile themes, sharply drawn conflict, positive characters and a melodramatic plot. The combination of these elements has resulted, on the negative side, in tragedies that are not too revolting in theme, and not too subtle and psychological in their action and exposition. On the positive side, the central characters have courage and conviction, and they fight heroically in their losing struggles. The melodramatic element is designed to make them dramatic enough to be understood and appreciated by the average audience rather than the sophisticated theatregoer."[4]

[2] R. Edmonds, *Six Plays for a Negro Theatre*, Boston, 1934, p. v.
[3] Edmonds, *op. cit.*, p. 111.
[4] *Ibid.*

THE LITTLE THEATRE MOVEMENT

In his "Bad Man," Randolph Edmonds has chosen a shanty in a factory town for his locale. The inhabitants of the shanty are sawmill workers and their families, ranging from sincere Christians to hardened criminals of the gambling and habitually drinking type. Many of these hard living characters are murderers and escaped convicts, illiterate, though possessed of keen, native wit. The hero, who is leader of a vicious gang, is one of this type. And to disobey one of his slightest whims swiftly results in death. Nothing seems to halt this tyrannical despotism, until a young, vivacious girl prevails upon him to prevent the slaughter of a member of the gang who has committed some trifling offense. Meanwhile, a mob of hoodlums forms to lynch a member of the group, who is supposed to have killed a white man. Then, refusing to believe that any of his gang is guilty, he attacks the mob single-handed, and, like a martyr in a great cause, meets his death.

For the unfortunately pathetic plight of "Old man Pete," the playwright has selected a neatly furnished apartment in Harlem for the scene of action. To this gay, Negro community of Manhattan Island, Old Man Pete Collier and his aged wife, by request, went to pay their children a visit. But soon after their arrival, the parents became aware that the children did not welcome their presence. As a matter of fact, the parents not only consumed food and bedroom space which were quite an economic item in New York, but they were actually a bore in the riotous and tumultuous life of Harlem. Recognizing the cold reception on the part of the children, the "ole folks" started for home with an insufficient amount of clothing or money for transportation. Incapable of standing the bitter cold of northern weather, their bodies were found frozen in a park the following morning.

In "Nat Turner" the dramatist is concerned with the reproduction of an historical incident in connection with the Southampton insurrectionist, who, in 1831, stirred a group of slaves to such a pitch of frenzy that they turned on their masters, slaying them and their families. In their attempt to throw off the shackles of slavery, by death and destruction of their tormentors, Nat Turner and his band were soon overtaken and put to death. The writing and subsequent production of "Nat Turner" won for Randolph Edmonds a scholarship at the Yale School of Drama in 1934.

Another drama, "Breeders," the name of which suggests its theme, concerns itself with the raising of slaves in the same way in which hogs or cattle are produced. The master only wants healthy, fertile women to breed plenty of strong children to work on his plantation. Even though one of his female slaves is in love with a man of her own choice, the master tells her that she must marry another big, rough fellow forthwith. In her lover's anxiety to offset the impending forced marriage, he takes issue with the master and is slain. The maiden, in her bereavement over the death of her lover, drinks hemlock.

The most natural scene of "Bleeding Hearts," a play of eight characters, also takes place on a southern plantation. The master insists that a mother and wife, living in one of his shanties, and who is desperately ill, come up to the Big House to help his wife. Later the husband finds a minister and a small group of friends praying and singing over her. In his bereavement, he not only curses the sympathizers but reproves God, who he thinks, if He really existed would have prevented his wife's dying.

The sixth and last of Randolph Edmonds' book of plays, "The New Window," centers its theme on superstition. The heroine of the piece has certain superstitions which cause her to believe that bad luck will overtake her husband who earns his bread and butter by bootlegging. And strangely enough, as happens in all of Mr. Edmonds' plays, the hero meets with foul play.

Schools and colleges throughout the country have attested that Mr. Edmonds has done a meritorious job in the writing and publishing of this volume. It is rather infrequent to attend one of their programs, at which three or four plays are given, that one of Mr. Edmonds' plays is not on the bill.

Productions which have fired and stirred souls, without being forced to close after the first night or first week, have been those that dealt with vital, practical, everyday problems and experiences. Edmonds' plays are thus concerned. Hardly anyone would have the slightest notion that Marlowe's "Tamburlaine," or Shakespeare's "The Winter's Tale," or Ben Jonson's "Every Man in his Humor" could possibly thrive two years in the same theatre. But "Abie's Irish Rose," "Mulatto" and "Green Pastures" did just that. Edmonds, a student of drama, demonstrates in his own little naive plays that the modern author must present primarily a picture of life as it is, and not as it might be, or ought to be. The essential attributes of these plays may be summed up somewhat as follows: They have a single plot; that is, the story neither doubles nor trebles. The plays have struggle, conflict, and friction sustaining them from beginning to end and omitting non-dramatic elements, epic or lyric, oratorical or descriptive. Without using the soliloquy, except in "Nat Turner," a technique usually employed during the seventeenth, eighteenth, and nineteenth centuries, Edmonds is able to keep the interest of the play rising steadily from the beginning to the end.

On the other hand, the author does not sufficiently sympathize with his heroes; not that he should be inordinately sympathetic, but he certainly should not vanquish his heroes unless their actions, of themselves, bring about their downfall. Nat Turner started on a fool's errand, to be sure. His scheme of destroying slavery was even more fantastic than that of John Brown, but what shall be said about Old Man Pete? What offense had he been guilty of that was punishable by death? And finally, Edmonds seems to have an ulterior motive in writing his plays. His themes are threadbare. Granting that he may have had the deliberate intent of presenting a picture of life, one must conclude that his main purpose seems to be to garnish melodrama.

However, the efforts of Randolph Edmonds are worthy of high praise. In addition to teaching, writing, and producing plays, he has been producing students. Perhaps his most noteworthy product is Carlton Moss. Young Moss has a three-fold distinction: he can write, teach, and act. Leigh Whipper is convinced that Carlton Moss is the best and most prolific Negro script-writer in New York City.[5] For a season (1932-1933) he wrote and presented skits for the

[5] In a conversation with Leigh Whipper in November, 1937, the present writer heard him express his opinion of Moss in these exact words, "Moss is the best and most prolific writer in New York."

National Broadcasting System. When the rehabilita-
tion program was launched in Harlem, following the
first inauguration of the New Deal Administration,
Moss was chosen from a large group of candidates to
teach drama. And when the Federal Theatre project
began in New York, he became one of its moving and
versatile figures.

Inspired by the dramatic success of Charles Gilpin,
a small group of Cleveland amateurs decided to establish themselves as a permanent organization in
1923. The little club was all the more determined
and its enthusiasm greatly bolstered when Gilpin, who
was a top-ranking Negro actor, spoke to the group,
and emphasized the importance of a dignified organization. At that time the few zestful players hardly
did more than organize. Three years later, however,
the size and prestige of the club had developed to
such extent that a building was necessary if the movement were to go forward with any degree of success.
Hence, the group, now known as the Gilpin Players,
renovated a large building which has been used ever
since, except on the occasion of the presentation of
"Stevedore" the noted propaganda play. Then, the
city officials, failing in their attempt to dissuade the
group's giving the play, condemned the building as a
fire hazard.

Today, the organization is a respectable community-
enterprise, performing a civic function that is exten-
sively appreciated. In addition to producing folk
plays and pieces that have had Broadway runs, the
club has produced plays written within its rank. The
players are enjoying the right to feel proud of their
sixteen years of achievement. Their number has
steadily increased. The young and those who never

grow old have affiliated themselves. Unselfishly laboring, with no thought of financial reward, members have given their energy unreservedly. Those who demonstrate promise and talent are aided in the pursuance of organized training.

Among those who appeared in the early productions of the Ethiopian Art Theatre were players who subsequently became Broadway stars. Included in the charter membership were Laura Bowman, Evelyn Preer and Sidney Kirkpatrick. Their shows were considered smart and entertaining. Later, when the same players produced a burlesque version of "Comedy of Errors" in New York, they were a miserable failure. However, they again made a sudden flair with Ridgeley Torrence's "Rider of Dreams." Having at times appeared to be disbanded, the organization has had continuous interruptions.

Organized in 1937 by Langston Hughes, the Suitcase Theatre is a significant proletarian organization. Although it boasts of no top-ranking stars, it does have a conscientious group that are concerned with the oppression of their race. Accordingly, they have presented plays that express their reaction. The most significant of such plays is "Don't You Want To Be Free?" by its founder. So popular was the play for labor audiences when it was produced in April, 1938, that it was revived in September of 1938. Showing once a week, it had a run of two months.

Located in the West 135th Street Library, New York City, the theatre has its performances Sunday nights. When there is no play scheduled, outstanding artists of stage, screen and radio furnish entertainment. Having grown beyond its own expectation, the organization has employed Thomas Richardson, a trained and experienced man of the theatre, as executive director.

Organized in 1938 by a group of theatrical minded persons of Harlem were the Rose McClendon Players. When they officially opened with Arthur Kober's "Having a Wonderful Time," the press observed that if they continue to progress, the community theatre sought by the people of Harlem would not be far off. The audience laughed heartily at "Goodbye Again." *The New York Age* thought the performance was "superb." "Right Angle Triangle" was also widely acclaimed. *The Chicago Defender* stated that it "bordered on professionalism." *The New York Amsterdam News* commented, "Its handling is something to make both author and director proud." One of the fundamental aims of this Little Theatre seems to be to encourage and cultivate talent among Negro playwrights. The fact that the McClendon Players have announced four plays written by young Negro playwrights supports this assumption. The best two of this group are: "Joy Exceeding Glory," based on the Father Divine movement, by George Norford, and "Le Bourgeois Gentilhomme," a satire on the highbrow Negroes of Harlem, by Wilson Williams.

In 1935, Fannin S. Belcher of West Virginia State College organized a play tournament among the high schools of West Virginia. The objectives of the organization as stated by Belcher are: (1) "To raise the standards of dramatics in our high schools; (2) to cultivate in our students a more genuine enthusiasm for drama; (3) to promote the community use of dramatics as a valuable leisure-time entertainment."

In its first year of operation, twelve schools participated with the Dunbar High School of Fairmont winning first prize, presenting Francis Spencer's "Dregs." In 1936, fourteen schools supported the activity. Dunbar High School of Fairmont was again awarded first prize, with Dorothy Wilson's "The Whirlwind." Enthusiasm had developed to such extent by 1937 that fifteen plays were produced. Sumner High School of Parkersburg won the West Virginia's Players cup with Mae Barry's "The Mother Who Went Away." In the fourth year of the tournament, sixteen schools actively engaged. Garnet High School of Charleston was the winner, producing Guernsey Le Pelley's "Another Beginning." The 1939 tournament also produced sixteen plays. Kimball High School won, presenting "Thank You Doctor" by Gilbert Emery.

The Negro Intercollegiate Dramatic Association, which includes seven colleges, was founded in 1930 by Randolph Edmonds, at that time director of drama at Morgan College. These colleges are: Morgan College of Baltimore, Maryland; Howard University of Washington, D. C.; Virginia State College of Ettrick, Virginia; Virginia Union University of Richmond, Virginia; Shaw University of Raleigh, North Carolina; Lincoln University of Oxford, Pennsylvania; and Agricultural and Technical College of Greensboro, North Carolina. Institutions winning first honors receive $50.00 in cash. Those winning second place receive $25.00. Edmonds was president of the association until he was succeeded by Arthur P. Davis, who has held the office ever since.

The Intercollegiate Dramatic Association was founded in North Carolina in 1933. All of the thirteen colleges of the state have participated except a "university" in the southwestern part of the state.

THE LITTLE THEATRE MOVEMENT

The reasons given for not supporting the movement by that institution are (1) there would be no opportunity to present classical plays, and (2) there would be too much responsibility upon the institution serving as host. But the other institutions of the State with a progressive ambition have forged ahead and achieved appreciation, cultural entertainment and cultivation of dramatic talent. During its first three years of operation the tournament was on a competitive basis; however, in 1936 decisions and prizes were eliminated. Since that time, the colleges, still possessing a decided stimulation, have looked forward to the annual event with keen interest.

Largely because of the efforts of Clinton L. Blake, principal of a Charlotte, North Carolina, high school, the High School Dramatic Association has developed in size, enthusiasm, and community importance. The association is composed of 36 high schools divided into two units—one in the eastern part of the state and the other in the western. These units operate separately until the best production of each division, as judged by competent critics, is chosen. These two productions come together in Raleigh and vie for first honors. The school winning in this contest is considered the State Champion.

While Atlanta University does not emphasize drama during its fall and winter sessions, it does afford interested students an opportunity to see and engage in five plays during its Summer Theatre. Aside from encouraging the writing of plays, another purpose of the Summer Theatre, according to Miss Anne Margaret Cooke, director, "is to encourage interest in dramatics and enable the summer school community to enjoy a group of well-acted and well produced

133

plays.'' The company is composed of members of the faculty and students who have had some previous experience in the theatre. With the possible exception of Miss Lillian Welch Voorhees (white), Miss Cooke has a better dramatic background than any person working in Negro schools. She has had three years of training in the Yale School of Drama, one year at the Chicago Art Theatre, one year at the American Laboratory Theatre, and one year at the Pauley-Oukrainsky School of Ballet.

While the writer was making a personal survey of dramatic departments of Negro colleges, he observed that Talladega College has the best equipped workshop that came within his purview. Miss Lillian Voorhees, director of the players, courteously took him through a monument of art. Possessing a bachelor and master's degree in drama, Miss Voorhees is well aware of the essentials of drama, and her house of preparation attests the assumption. The shop is a credit to the players. Productions by the Talladega Players have included the entire range of diversity. They present everything from Shakespeare and Ibsen to folk plays of Edmonds and Green. The director likes to present a Shakespearean play once in every four years so that each student body may have an opportunity of seeing a play of the master.

The Neighborhood Players, under the direction of Montgomery Gregory, Atlantic City, New Jersey, were founded by Dr. Mario Bedio, Mexican brain specialist, who had studied at the Russian Art Theatre. Gregory, who had been director of the Howard University Players, entered upon educational work in Atlantic City in 1925. Soon after his arrival, he succeeded the Mexican physician, who had divided his efforts between the white and the colored players. Strangely enough, Bedio had been interested in a diversity of plays—ranging from folk plays to those of Christopher Marlowe. Gregory, on the other hand, thinks Negroes should do best what they know best. Accordingly, he has leaned backwards with the Paul Green specie.

The frank fact remains that the Neighborhood Players sustain a membership of a hundred young men and women, who are intensely interested in learning and disseminating drama. Cooperation still exists between them and the whites. Professionals and stock players are often called in for advice and to speak to the group. During the summer, the Players read and criticise plays as well as see and analyze pieces presented in the city by stock companies.

The Little Theatre of Columbus, Ohio, is also a reality. In 1934, Thomas Poag, a former student of Randolph Edmonds, matriculated at Ohio State University to pursue graduate work in drama. Shortly after his arrival in Columbus, Poag organized a little theatre in the basement of the Spring Street Y. M. C. A. Within three months, the theatre had a progressive membership that was not only producing but writing plays. The writer, who was recently in the city was invited to attend one of the rehearsals. To his satisfying amazement a postal clerk, with his wife and daughter, was directing a play written by himself. Notwithstanding the youth of the Columbus movement, the Players have presented in the churches of the City successful performances of folk plays.

In 1937, Blyden Jackson, instructor in the Madison Junior High School organized a play tournament in Louisville, Kentucky. Unable to receive an audience during the first year, Jackson was allowed to have the plays presented in a local theatre before or after a regular show. As soon as interest was aroused he withdrew from the theatre. Although the movement is state-wide only Louisville schools have won medals to date.

The majority of Negro colleges have not yet manifested any appreciable interest in dramatics. Various and sundry reasons are given as the cause, some of which are lack of administrative interest, lack of trained instructors, lack of funds, lack of talent, and lack of rehearsal facilities. In two instances, it was noted that the administrators used the dramatic fund for football equipment.

The Dillard University Theatre under the direction of Randolph Edmonds is developing rapidly. The University is encouraging students of promise in tangible ways. Edmonds has had years of experience and training in writing and directing play; moreover, he has studied at the Yale School of Drama.

Officials of Knoxville College say they wish to emphasize the dramatic talent of their students, indicating as much by cataloguing seven courses. The directors, however, seem to have had little or no organized training in the field of drama. The writer arrived at Knoxville College just as the curtain was about to rise on a one-act comedy, which was poorly directed. Fisk University's claim to dramatic renown rests upon the fame of its Jubilee Singers. LeMoyne College of Memphis, Tennessee, has a department of speech and dramatic art, conducted by a person trained in English. The speech emphasis there has been on debating. North Carolina State College at Durham has had a trained teacher of drama for the past six years. The person preceding Miss Zora Neal Hurston, present incumbent, held a bachelor's and master's degree in speech from the University of Southern California. Miss Hurston has a national reputation as dramatist and novelist. Under the direction of Miss Anne Margaret Cooke, Spelman College has an organized department of drama. Miss Cooke, who is also director of the Atlanta University Summer Theatre, has developed a drama conscious group at Spelman.

SUMMARY

The Negro as playwright has not succeeded to the extent that the Negro as actor has succeeded. In the writing of his plays, the Negro has not kept foremost before his mind a commercial goal. It augurs well for the Negro playwright, however, that he has made definite advancement as an amateur, writing for players in schools, colleges and Little Theatres which have been springing up in most of the states of the Union. In regard to the Little Theatre the Negro's effort has been vigorous and stimulating, as evidenced by the contributions of Willis Richardson and Randolph Edmonds.

CHAPTER IX

Dance and Jazz: A Folk Art Contribution

That modern dancing is unmistakably of Negro origin, bearing its imprint from the Atlantic to the Pacific coasts, throughout Europe and to some extent in the Orient, students of the art have agreed. Perhaps no other form of entertainment has been modified more since the Great War, than has dancing. With the exception of the "waltz," and to a small extent the "two-step," the formal and precise dances of a quarter century ago were formal, punctilious, and ceremonious—hardly more than rituals.

Now that formality has been discarded, because of Negro influence, the old and the young enjoy the merrymaking, the reason being that the couple now dance as one, moved by individual response. Each person is influenced and governed by his own mood and that of his partner. A couple may now merely walk around, dance slowly, fast, do particularly fascinating steps, or any other type that appeals to their immediate fancy. Vernon Castle and his wife of London, England, who had seen these dances of twos done by American Negroes, were so impressed and captivated by the charm of these dances that they had them reproduced on the stage in 1914. Americans admired these dances and were somewhat surprised when Castle informed them that he had first seen these dances done by American Negroes.

One of the best known of these dances originated in

DANCE AND JAZZ

Charleston, S. C., in 1920, and forthwith was introduced to the stage by Miller and Lyles as "The Charleston." Thereupon, moving picture and stage firms sent their dancing instructors to Charleston to get first hand information of the new fad that was taking the country by storm. As soon as it made its appearance on stage and screen, "The Charleston" spread throughout the country and even to foreign countries.

In 1928 revelers at the Savoy Ball Room in Harlem dedicated to the flight hero a "dance hit," known as "The Lindy Hop." When Colonel Charles A. Lindbergh made his flight to Paris in 1927, he was hailed as the hero of the age; the Lindbergh fame spread all over the world, and almost everything assumed his name. Whites have marveled at the dance named for him, and have had it taught to them by Negro dance teachers; but because of its difficulties of performance, it has not been widely taken up by the whites. A most facetious spectacle is to see whites trying to do the dance. Their efforts are no more successful than they are when whites attempt to sing Negro spirituals. Without Negro performance both are colorless and flat.[1]

Two other dances are the "Suzy-Q" and the "Big Apple." The latter originated in the home of "The Charleston," and studio authorities have sent dance teachers to South Carolina to acquire its technique.[2] The "Tango," too, is of Negro origin, although it originated with the Cubans and came by way of Paris to the United States. James Weldon Johnson reminds

[1] This statement was taken from lectures delivered by J. W. Johnson, New York University, November, 1937.

[2] The New York *Amsterdam*, March 30, 1928.

us in his lectures on Negro Folk Arts that wherever one goes, be it Russia, England, France, Japan or the capitals of Africa, one sees distinct traces of the American Negro dance.

In tap-dancing the Negro is the greatest attraction on the stage. In this sphere he has few competitors. It is now generally agreed that Bill Robinson is the outstanding tap-dancer of the present time. Although he is 61 years old he, nevertheless, teaches Shirley Temple. He has also recently tutored Jeni Legon in the art of dancing. In November, 1937, Doris Duke was so impressed with his interpretation of the "Suzy-Q" that she engaged him for a series of private lessons which he gave her at the Cotton Club, with Cab Calloway and his hi-de-ho band providing the music. In addition to instruction in the "Suzy-Q" Robinson taught her steps in "Truckin," a 1936 Negro "breath-taker."[3]

After the production of Lew Leslie's "Black Birds of 1933," which made its first appearance at the Apollo Theatre, December 2, of that year, an anonymous critic wrote in part, "Bill Robinson saves a floundering show. He is the one master of style. Without wasting energy or time or directing attention to anything else except his virtuoso feet, he devotes his efforts to tap-dancing, which is a form of physical exercise he has transplanted into magic. He is a poet when his feet are pattering. But when his equipment consists of nothing but a smartly tailored three-piece suit, a derby hat, and a diamond ring, he is good enough for any student of the fine arts, for Bill is a master of style. He has reduced his act to its essentials. Without any suggestion of trickery or cleverness,

[3] *The Afro-American*, December 30, 1937, p. 12.

he keeps his feet tapping a light rhythm that quickens your pulse.''

Robinson has been engaged in the art of dancing for a half century. He has made that art a part of his personality. He dances without apparent effort or exertion. In this respect, he has surpassed most of the other artists who swing their arms and legs frantically, bending, turning, breathing hard, perspiring—in short, exerting stupendous effort. Bill ''Bojangles'' Robinson, when he dances, remains cool, calm, and collected, as it were. With so little effort does he dance that he scarcely soils his immaculately laundered linen. There is no evidence of strain; and there is always the indication of his ability to put more into the act.

That he is master of this dramatic art was evidenced January 21, 1938, at the Cotton Club, New York City, when he was crowned King of Actors on Broadway.[4] Robinson was awarded this honor as a result of a popular straw vote conducted by the New York Daily *Mirror*. From this poll, he received the largest number of votes of any actor on Broadway. Present to witness the ceremony were stars of radio, screen and stage.

Writing on ''The Negro Dance, Under European Eyes,'' André Levison, French critic observed, ''Negro music having conquered the public, Negro ragtime having become worthy of the most serious consideration, jazz is henceforth admitted into the hierarchy of the arts; and although it has only been a little while since it was the butt of the press and public, time is at hand when it will provide worthy subject matter for a doctor's thesis at the Sorbonne.

[4] New York *Daily Mirror*, January 22, 1938.

"Since it is the cradle of the prototype, jazz must be taken seriously. The student of esthetics may consider its intrinsically artistic value, the moralist its effect on civilization, and organic phenomenon; and as a sympton of epidemic contagion of society it should appease the pathologist."[5]

In further describing the Revue Nègre at the Champs Elysées, M. Levison observed that in the Negro dance like most folk dances from the Russian *hopak* to the Scotch reel, the step is based on a direct and audible expression of the rhythm. The Negro dance is all the more impressive because of its staccato, rapid and clear articulation, surpassing the *pas de ballet*. The occasion on which Levison wrote was the appearance of Josephine Baker and Florence Mills in Paris. The two Afro-Americans had been well received in that city. Parisian critics admitted that their new step and sense of rhythm were a genuine contribution to the art of dancing. The two colored performers were not referred to merely as dancing girls, but, in the language of the French press "as an African Enos and a black Venus that haunted Baudelaire." Levison also made such allusions to Josephine Baker's artistry as: "a gushing stream of rhythm," "bold dislocations," "springing movements," "carnal magnificence," "impulsive vehemence," and one with "symmetry of pattern."[6]

"This Negro ragtime, executed with such unimaginable dexterity," Levison continues, "positively dazzles European audiences. This dancing with its automaton, its marvelous flexibility and rhythmic fantasy

[5] "The Negro Dance Under European Eyes," *The Theatre Arts Monthly*, May, 1927, pp. 282-287.
[6] *Ibid.*, p. 287.

is as impossible for us to reproduce as it is astounding for us to watch. Here we see ourselves in the presence of an innate art, not a conscious art.''[7]

It is believed by John Banting, who has studied the step of the Harlem Negro as well as that of the native African, that this ragtime or jazz was derived from the Negro's ancestors on the continent of Africa. He emphatically denies the assumption that it had its origin with the American Negro, or that the latter has acquired it through training. Rather, he assumes as a result of prolonged study, that the rhythm of the ritualistic dances performed by the natives are similar in step to those of the American ''Charleston,'' ''Shimmy,'' ''Black Bottom,'' and the ''Lindy Hop,'' done on Harlem stages and dance halls, and in certain evangelical churches. He is also of the opinion that given a lively orchestra and a sympathetic audience to appreciate their delicate finesse, Negroes could perform without previous practice as smoothly and as rhythmically as a practiced professional.[8] Although differing from James Weldon Johnson who does not believe that the Negro is a born actor and dancer, Banting does agree that the Negro dances have been taken over step by step by the whites. This contention is borne out by the fact that, in 1927, George White used ''The Charleston'' on Broadway and gave the impression that he himself had originated it.

In 1925, the ''Shimmy'' which originated in a Negro locale was taken from that sphere, introduced and popularized among the whites by Gilda Grey. As

[7] Levison, *op. cit.*, p. 287.

[8] John Banting, The Dancing of Harlem, *Negro Anthology*, by Nancy Cunard, published by Nancy Cunard. London: 1934, p. 322.

popular as the dance was, it did not last, because it was considered by polite society as vulgar. In going through the motions of the "Shimmy," the dancer's body would quaver, vibrate with a slight tremulous movement, shake and leap at the torso. In fact, it was considered vulgar in the extreme.

While the rhythm of the dance is found wherever Negroes carouse, it is mostly from the Harlem dance floors that whites attempt to capture the art. On these floors, Harlem's younger set gather nightly to do their graceful rhythm, and forget the day's toil by finding pleasure in a graceful movement, which comes to them impromptu. The white observer gasps in astonishment as he gazes upon a couple that wheels around in each other's embrace—dashing, speeding, uniting and disuniting in a whirling movement and interweaving again and again in exact fashion. Such a performance may take place in one, two, or a combination of several dances, with a pronounced limp on every third or fourth beat, and displays a series of acrobatic details. When the dancers' applauding fails to bring forth another encore from the orchestra, they go gaily to their boxes and lodges.

A recent dance, too, "The Big Apple," which originated in the deep South in the beginning of 1937, was filmed in December of that year for Paramount's "Thrill of a Life Time." Rumor of America's latest dance which permits the dancer to express himself and his emotions singularly in numerous ways, reached the film capital just as "Thrill of a Life Time" was to be produced; thereupon Paramount sent an agent to the South to observe the new dance. The agent, finding that the South was widely enthusiastic over the dance, suggested that it be included in the picture.[9]

[9] *Theatre Arts Monthly*, July, 1933, pp. 486-487.

DANCE AND JAZZ

A 1939 thriller was the dance known as the "Jitter-bug," which is traced from the barbaric African dances to the primitive antics of current times. A form of Swing closely related to the "Rug Cutting," a 1937 hit, the "Jitterbug" is a fast, jumping "jamboree." It is the dance that makes one wonder why the building does not tumble down. Officials have threatened to condemn buildings because of the tremendous commotion associated with the "Jitter-bug." Turning, weaving, twisting, spinning the part-ner, cutting capers, all are done at dangerous speed. It is the dance that created such a sensation in Har-lem, the home of its birth, that it was immediately adapted by a Swing crazed nation. It is the whirl featured in the Savoy Theatre, at the New York 1939 World's Fair that astounds thousands who attend the amusement area. It is the dance that enabled Connie Hill and Russell Williams to win the Harvest Moon contest in competition with hundreds of white couples at Long Island, New York, and to earn the plaudits of Brooklyn when they later starred in New York City.

Ragtime dancing had its origin on the lower Miss-issippi, and was first shown at the Chicago Fair in 1893. The rag-songs were carefully composed by Negroes, perhaps the most notable of whom was Augustus L. Davis, who sang them all over the coun-try.[10]

The first jazz band of which there is any record was heard at Proctor's Theatre, New York, in 1905, and was made up of various instruments, played by a group of Memphis students. The band was unique in

[10] Johnson, *op. cit.*

that it danced and played as well as sang simultaneously. The conductor of the orchestra, for the first
time, sprightly cut capers, danced grotesquely, and
sang comic songs—all of which were interspersed with
witticism. In other words, the conductor played the
role of a jester by bantering the members of the
orchestra. To add to this flair of entertainment, Buddy
Gilmore introduced the trap-drum: a combination of
instruments pieced together as one, producing several
sounds in a trip-trap manner.[11]

From then on, the American folk, especially those
who enjoyed popular music regarded jazz as something
soothing and pleasant—not vile, ignoble, or sordid. In
the category of ragtime entertainment belong Fletcher
Henderson, Jimmie Lunceford, Cab Calloway, Claude
Hopkins, and Duke Ellington. The last mentioned is
an outstanding composer and orchestra leader, who,
by an international poll conducted by an English
theatrical paper, was voted the leader in his field for
the year 1936.

The New York Daily *Mirror* for November 15, 1937,
featured the life story of Cab Calloway, one of the
most versatile characters in jazz. The account in the
newspaper stated, among other things, that the King
of Jazz was born to a Negro lawyer who died when
Cab Calloway was seven years old. His mother taught
school music. Cab sold newspapers—"I could yell so
loud you could hear me easy for three blocks," he said.
"I also sang in the Presbyterian church choir. I had
a big voice."[12]

Cab attended the Douglass High School in Baltimore
where he played in all of the sports, and was captain

[11] J. W. Johnson, *Black Manhattan*. New York: Alfred
Knopf, 1930, p. 120.
[12] *The New York Daily Mirror*, November 15, 1937.

of the basketball team. A man, hearing him sing in Baltimore, gave him a job with an orchestra as singing tap-drummer. His sister, Blanche Calloway, who was in musical comedy, took him to Chicago where he did small musical parts. While taking a pre-law course by day and playing with Louis Armstrong at night, his talent soon became recognized. After his appearance in Chicago, he toured Europe. Even Scotland welcomed his hi-de-ho jazz.

With his colored orchestra, he has toured America several times. Those occasions have not always been pleasant. Once the crowd became unruly at Durham, North Carolina, and he had to pack up and leave. On another occasion, it is said that the son of a local police chief in Florida threw a coca cola bottle at Cab, missed and hit the drummer, splitting his head open. However, Cab was not too greatly disturbed, and he kept his orchestra playing and won the crowd, although he later said, "I wanted to run."

Cab was at his wits' end in Texas when he saw a sign reading, "Nigger don't let sun set on you in this county." His was the first tawny orchestra ever to tour Texas. Scared though he was, he was the personality to make Texas love him and his jazz. The Southern Methodsit University "Mustangs" purchased the seating capacity of the theatre in which he played for three nights. A year later, in 1936, he was invited back to Texas to play at the Texas Centennial. His hi-de-ho music had taken like magic.[13]

Meanwhile, Bessie Smith, as related by Van Vechten, had blazed the Blues' trail. He wrote for *Vanity Fair*,[14] "Her face was beautiful, with the rich

[13] *Ibid.*, November 15, 1937.
[14] Carl Van Vechten, "Negro Blues," *Vanity Fair*, November 26, 1926, p. 36.

ripe beauty of southern darkness. . . . She began her strange rites in a voice full of shouting, moving and praying, and suffering a wild, rough Ethiopian voice, harsh and volcanic, released between rouged lips, the singer swaying slightly to the rhythm.''

An editorial in *Vanity Fair* stated, ''Soon, doubtless, the homely Negro songs of love sickness, known as the 'Blues' will be better known and appreciated by white audiences.''[15] At the very moment Bessie Smith was endeared to many a jazz lover, as was evidenced by the fact that she was earning $9,000 a month.

When Bessie Smith died in November, 1937, the Columbia Phonograph Company was reminded of her popularity during the golden 1920's, and issued a Bessie Smith Album, containing re-pressings of six of the 80 records she made between 1922-1929.

Time Magazine observed at her death that ''she brought the blues and jazz North, lived to see strict blues singing yield popularity to the sophisticated torch singing typified by the art of Ethel Waters. But Bessie Smith left her mark on jazz . . . Fletcher Henderson, who played the piano for her 'Weeping Willow Blues' accompanied by Louis Armstrong on the cornet, calls this the greatest blues record ever made. 'Careless Love' is W. C. Handy's arrangement of what is almost a U. S. folk song. 'Trombone Charley' is a classic . . . Only three of the twelve sides in Bessie Smith's Album are devoted to Broadway songs: 'Muddy Water,' 'Alexander's Ragtime Band,' 'There'll Be a Hot Time in the Old Town Tonight'.''[16]

W. C. Handy, the man who has come to be known

[15] *Vanity Fair*, November, 1926, p. 43.
[16] *Time*, November 2, 1937.

as the father of the Blues, was born November 16, 1873, in Florence, Alabama, the son and grandson of Methodist ministers.[17] In 1909, Handy aided Edward H. Crump, later a Congressman, in the campaign for Mayor of Memphis.[18] This assistance consisted largely in writing a campaign song, which came to be known as the "Memphis Blues."[19] The Blues' vogue, which swept the country, prompted Handy's remark, "The Negro invented jazz, and the white folks made an industry of it." After selling the publishing rights of the Memphis Blues for $100, he composed another familiar number known as the "St. Louis Blues." This latter composition has placed him in comfortable circumstances, for whether these Blues are programmed in the United States, Europe, Australia or South America, he receives royalty. The chorus of the St. Louis Blues is:

> Got de St. Louis Blues, jes blue as ah can be,
> Dat man got a heart like a rock in the sea,
> Or else he wouldn't get so far from me.

The term "Blues" has no derivative. It simply suddenly appeared. It is to be noted that "Blues" expresses the mood and feeling of an individual. Because of its Negro association, it was for a number of years looked upon disdainfully. But an avalanche of praise accompanied it with the appearance of "Krazy Kat," in 1923, and Gershwin's "Rhapsody in Blue," in 1924. In 1921, James Weldon Johnson rightly assumed that Handy's Blues would come to have tremendous influence upon modern music.

[17] W. C. Handy, *Blues; An Anthology*, 1926.
[18] *Ibid.*
[19] *Encyclopedia Britannica*, 14th Edition, III, 756-757.

THE NEGRO AND THE DRAMA

The cheerful philosophy of the illiterate Negro expressed through song, has brought to the composer of the Blues, international fame. The leading newspapers of the country ofttimes honored him with editorials. Countless languages have made arrangements of his music. In his honor the Handy Park was dedicated in Memphis, March 31, 1931. An official of the city said to Handy, "We want you to know what the City of Memphis thinks of you." On that occasion one of the biggest parades ever witnessed in the City turned out to do him honor. Appreciative of his contribution the St. Louis Music Association presented him a plaque, its achievement award, on the occasion of the Eighteenth Annual Convention of the National Association of Negro Musicians.

"Swing" has had its rise also recently. "Swing" is a combination of (a) two-step rhythm, with a double accent, (b) fox trot rhythm, (c) jungle hopping and (d) syncopated melody. In addition, it embraces the music of the African, the South American, the Indian and the American whites. Originating among the revelers of the Savoy Ballroom of Harlem in 1937, it was soon brought to the notice of the general public, Benny Goodman became interested in the fad during the winter of 1937-1938. Upon further study he found it good and fine. His orchestra, however, was unable to perform it satisfactorily; whereupon Goodman provided space in his orchestra for one or two Negro Swing artists. The appearance of Negroes in a white orchestra was unique. If Goodman experienced any chagrin, he was compensated with subsequent popularity, for when his Swing orchestra appeared at the high-brow Paramount Theatre in the spring of 1939, it created a sensation that will long live in the memory of those who heard and saw the performers. The audience that had gathered to see a show could not restrain itself, and, as *Life* illustrated, finally succumbed to their emotions using the aisle of a theatre for leaping and frisking, to the tune of Jimmy Mundy's arrangements.

Swing Music has brought a flock of instrumentalists and singers to the front rank. Ella Fitzgerald composed "A-Tisket-A-Tasket," the song which made her famous. She has regularly appeared on radio programs. Before that she was popular with jitterbug. She has played at the Paramount with Chick Webb. Her beautiful voice and natural ability enable her to put her songs over in a way that is as charming as it is different. Should one question her versatility, one need only to observe these lines:

> A-tisket-a-tasket
> A brown and yellow basket
> I wrote a letter to my mama
> And on the way I dropped it.

Not only was this song an overnight hit, but was also responsible for a cycle of nursery rhyme hits.

Maxine Sullivan had her Swing start in Pittsburgh, doing small parts. Going to New York during the summer of 1936, she had within seven months grown rapidly in public favor, and captivated Americans of a Swing-conscious mood. Whether in musical comedies, in night clubs or on radio programs, she has received enthusiastic plaudits. Often referred to as the Queen of Swing, she has been featured by countless orchestras, including that of Noble Sissle, who thinks she is sensational. She appeared at Lewisohn Stadium July 11, 1939, on the George Gershwin Memorial Concert, and sang a number of Gershwin's favorite compositions, thereby increasing her popularity.

Other Swing stars, who have been cheered by the general public during the past two years, are Edna Mae Harris, Hazel Scott, Sara Turner, June Richmond, Slam Stewart and Slim Gaillard, authors of "Flat Foot Flugie," Ethel Moses, Dolores Brown and Anne Wiggins Brown, who was unusually effective in the musical extravaganza, "In Virginia."

Jimmie Lunceford and his famous Swing orchestra seem to have a type of Swing that is so fascinating that it appeals to nearly everybody everywhere, for his organization is the most widely traveled of all swing orchestras. Moreover, he has delighted Broadway audiences with music that seems different. The late Chick Webb rose rapidly as a Swing artist during his thirty short years. Andy Kirk and his orchestra are as well known in Chicago as they are in New York or Boston. His appearance in Chicago in June, 1939, called for a four weeks' stay at the Chicago Savoy. His orchestra, which featured Mary Lou Williams at the piano, during the Chicago assignment, broadcast three nights a week over the Columbia system, on a coast-to-coast network. Louis Armstrong will be remembered as a great swing artist. Radios, night clubs, and dance halls have sought his brand of merrymaking. Noble Sissle is leaning heavily toward Swing, in that he has featured Swing artists in his band. Cab Calloway is mixing Swing with his rousing hi-de-ho. Ed Sullivan, Hollywood columnist for the *Daily News*, says that Erskine Hawkins has the "greatest crop of trumpeteers." Be that as it may, his orchestra is as popular in Hollywood as it is in Harlem's Savoy Ballroom.

DANCE AND JAZZ

On September 10, 1938, when Paul Whiteman's selection of an All American Swing Band appeared in *Collier's Weekly*, six of his twenty-six artists were Negroes. They are Bennie Carter, Chu Berry, Roy Eldridge, Louis Armstrong, Art Tatum and Eddie Smith. In making his selection, Whiteman said, "Every man I'm picking except one, who is blind, is a fine reader of music, a man who has mastered the fundamentals, and who has gone beyond that technique to add something of his own."

NIGHT CLUBS

Definitely interwoven in the jazz of the Negro is his jollity and mirth which gush forth in night clubs. Every American city that has a considerable Negro population has a Negro night club. It is in Harlem, however, that they thrive as a big business, employing hundreds of workers as entertainment makers, and others as servants from dish-washers to doormen and proprietors. Since polite society of Park and Fifth Avenues has decided that these night clubs are not nefarious caverns in which only sensual lewdness abounds, they have become the rendezvous for New Yorkers, and out-of-town visitors.[20] Dignitaries, business folk, school teachers, et cetera, are witnesses of this sort of light and pleasant entertainment which is supposed to release inhibitions. Asked why they frequent these clubs, these visitors immediately reply that only the Negro is capable of throwing off all restraint and inhibition, and of performing according to the urges of his own emotions. The Negro entertainer does not desire to be repellent or odious; neither does

[20] James Weldon Johnson, *Black Manhattan*. New York: Alfred Knopf, 1930, pp. 179-180.

he desire to repress his exhilaration and animation,
lest he should offend the timid. Being in his own
locale, and responsible only to his own race, giving
them the kind of entertainment they desire, he has
no qualms of conscience.

Despite the fact that entertainers are not con-
strained in their exhibitions, even the more retiring
and faint-hearted ladies will hardly be affronted, or
disquieted. Respectable citizens go for fun, joviality
and hilarity, which they themselves may help to
furnish by dancing; or they may be emotionally
soothed from hearing the latest song hits, seeing
snappy dancing or chorus girls, and hearing subtly
told anecdotes.

The evening, or early morning as it more often is,
is all the more enjoyable because the patron has an opportunity of getting away from himself, and is under
the protection of bouncers, doormen, and officers of
the law, as he dines and sips cocktails in high spirits
to the tune of an enlivened orchestra.

It is understood also that this entertainment is very
expensive to the average working man of small salary.
Because of this expensiveness, he has to make his
trips to these places of amusements rather in-
frequently.[21]

[21] An illustration is the experience of a teacher, whose name
we shall not call, working for a Master's degree at Columbia
University. He decided to write his thesis on the Harlem night
clubs. Deciding to cover the swanky resorts first, he went
to Connie's Inn where he was perched back in a corner, for the
center and near-center of the floor, save space of entertainment,
were reserved for those whom the management knew to be
lavish and prodigal in their spending. However, keeping within
the spirit of the occasion, he thought he should, at least, drink
a five cent bottle of soda water, which even at a night club
would not cost more than a quarter of a dollar. After sitting
there for a half hour, he began to realize that his presence
would not be appreciated unless he tipped, drank and ate with
a relish. Upon receiving his check, he was alarmed at seeing a

DANCE AND JAZZ

Summary

The American dance as it has developed, and is presently practiced, has been influenced by the Negro. Prior to the adaptation of the Negro dance, the dance of the whites was formal and ceremonious. After the World War interest was manifested in the Negro dance because of its fascination and flexibility. One can hardly be surprised that many white students have studied dancing under Negro teachers. With the Negro, dancing is an art; whereas with white people dancing is an amusement.

For the one who can appreciate the beauty of Negro jazz, with its delicate humor, there is pleasure and exhilaration in its jungle rhythm and claptraps. This ragtime which has captured European and American audiences was born in the Negro's locale. The steps have been periodically modified, but the rhythms are very similar to the ritualistic dances performed by the African. One can hardly wonder that John Banting, an exponent of the African origin of the dance, concludes that as a test of the Negro's inherent jazz tendency, the Negro can perform artistically without the slightest preparation.

bill of $6.50 for nothing more tangible than a five cent bottle of ginger ale. Exorbitant to be sure, the waiter agreed but the thesis material seeker was also advised that beside himself, he had to pay cover-charge for a lady, even though he had brought none, since it was customary that only men with escorts were admitted. Moreover, the waiter was looking for a dollar tip from the parsimonious gentleman, notwithstanding the fact that he had not given the girl who danced at his table one. By giving the check girl only fifty cents, he was able to get out with having spent the miserly sum of $9.50, which included taxi expense back to the campus. Needless to say he did not so much as write the introduction to his proposed thesis of night club life. It is variously stated that to entertain a party of four which is the smallest party that could get the most out of the occasion, it would, spending conservatively, cost between $60.00 and $75.00.

CHAPTER X

NEGRO DRAMA IN MOVING PICTURES AND RADIO

When one inquires as to why the Negro has not come to the fore in moving pictures, the answer immediately given is that Hollywood producers are more concerned with box-office patronage than they are with advancement of art. Liberal minded persons of the East and West occasionally appreciate artistic entertainment regardless as to who furnishes it, but the attitude in parts of the South is different. Films, to be a financial success, must be sold in every section of the nation. Where prejudice abounds, boycott prevails, whether it be in radio, moving picture or other forms of entertainment.

When Ethel Waters, one of the nation's stars, was employed by an oil company to sing Negro blues over the National Broadcasting Company's network, protests came from Mississippi to the effect that unless her programs were discontinued, the petroleum customers of that state would boycott the firm.[1] There are southern folk who will not tolerate Negro entertainment that springs from southern soil. "Mulatto," with its scenes laid in Georgia, and which concerns itself with a code of ethics that deprives illegitimate children of their inalienable rights, was threatened with being stopped by process of law, in New York City, because of the reaction of a Georgia senator.[2] In New York,

[1] Norfolk *Journal and Guide*, December 20, 1935, p. 10.
[2] The New York *Times*, September 6, 1935.

"Mulatto," was a success for two years; but in Philadelphia it was not even permitted to be played.

However disturbing the foregoing facts may be, during the past decade, the Negro has had a degree of success in moving pictures. In earlier days, a Negro actor could have but a very minor part on the screen. However, the screening of "The Emperor Jones," and "The Green Pastures" was the beginning of a change for the better.

Likewise, the more recent production of the screen play, "Imitation of Life," from the novel by Fannie Hurst, indicates a change in popular attitude. This play which has been acclaimed by thousands of readers and theatre-goers, is the story of some of the glaring inconsistencies of American life. Though it has a double plot—that of a mulatto girl attempting to cross the color line, and that of the great mother-love for the daughter—the writer is primarily interested in the Negro phase of the plot. The plot takes a turn for the worse when the Negro woman, Deliliah, played by Louise Beavers, is given many heart aches by her mulatto daughter, Peola, who, after growing up, becomes aware that she can not secure and hold a job because of her color; nor can she enjoy the social privileges accorded the white race because of one insuperable obstacle—her black mother.

"Life Goes On," a graphic episode of native Negro life, also featured Louise Beavers. She was by far the outstanding figure in the cast. The picture was produced by Million Dollars Production, Inc. It had a colorful premiere New Year's Day in 1938. Her best picture to date is "Reform School," in which she stars first as probation officer and later as superintendent. Upon ingratiating herself into the confidence of the boys, she is able to bring about sensational improvements. During Louise Beavers' eleven years in Hollywood, she has appeared on the screen 261 times. The work of Stephen Fetchett shows advance in this direction. It is reasonable to suppose that Stephen Fetchett is the ranking Negro screen actor in America. Moreover, he is internationally known through his pictures for his comical drollery. He is perhaps best known for his acting in "Hearts in Dixie." Ada Brown, who has replaced Bessie Smith as "Queen of the Blues," is also a good screen actress.

The nationally known Nina Mae McKinney, the first Negro girl to pass the film test in the Metro-Goldwyn-Mayer Company was featured in "Hallelujah" heading a number of artists.[3] This picture was produced at a cost of a million dollars, and was shown all over America and in the leading theatres in Europe. Nina McKinney saw the production as it was shown in Paris, Berlin and Monte Carlo. Beginning her career as a chorus girl with Lew Leslie's "Black Birds," she was chosen for "Hallelujah" by the producer, King Victor, despite keen competition with a hundred other girls. In addition to playing on the legitimate stage, she has played an important part in "Safe in Hell," a Warner Brothers production.[4]

Clarence Muse, noted screen actor, has been featured in more pictures than any other person of his race. Working for the leading studios of Hollywood, his services are constantly in demand.

In the summer of 1936, when Paul Robeson was selected to play the lead in "King Solomon's Mines,"

[3] *The Afro-American*, "About Nina May," November 18, 1937.
[4] *Ibid.*, the New York *Sun*, June 20, 1936.

such headlines as the following appeared in the dramatic sections of newspapers:[5]

"Paul Robeson holds spotlight again."
"Star of 'Sanders of the River' and 'Emperor Jones' Cast in Lead."
"Star Returns to Role of Sovereign of Tribe Kingdom."

The magnificent voice of Robeson was heard in "King Solomon's Mines" and in his portrayal of Umbopoa, pretender to the throne of Kukuana. In that picture, Robeson sang the Kukana song, the Song of the Mountains, and trek songs. They were composed by Mischa Spoliansky, writer of the musical scores for films starring Jan Kiepura, and other musical personages.

Critics are of the opinion that the characterization of Ralph Cooper in "Bargain with Bullets" ranks among the best colored performances that have been screened to date.[6] Charles C. Moskowitz, managing director of Loew's great chain of theatres, made theatrical history in November, 1937, when he affixed his signature to the contract to buy that first Hollywood all-Negro picture, "Bargain with Bullets," a drama of Harlem's underworld, with its colored criminal characters matching wits with astute and clever officers. Ralph Cooper, the noted master of ceremonies and tap-dancer of New York, does a splendid interpretation of the role of the killer (Moore), the flashy and dapper proprietor of a tavern, who becomes the brains of a desperate gang of fur thieves.

The all-colored cast of "Harlem on the Prairie," written in 1937 and played for the first time in 1938, has received much praise from critics. It is a western

---

[5] The New York *Sun*, July 20, 1936.
[6] The Amsterdam *News*, December 15, 1937.

production, featuring Connie Harris. Also doing
commendable roles in the play are Herbert Jeffries
and Maceo B. Sheffield, the latter taking the role of
the villain.

To William Nolte the press has been unanimous in
giving unstinted credit for the way in which he has
permitted the unfolding of Negro themes and characterization. It is often stated that Nolte considers
Louise Beavers as one of the great artists of the profession. Asked why he desires to direct Negro casts,
Nolte answered:

"I have always felt a deep interest in the race, partly
because their whole history has been persevering, with an
optimistic struggle for expression and success, also because they deserve the aid that could only come from experience gained already in the products of the major
studios that pioneered years ago in the infancy of motion
pictures."[7]

Aside from this point, Nolte's experience and observation had taught him, he asserted, that the Negro
is very apt at mimicry, natural in interpretation, and
that, since the advent of the sound pictures, he had
observed that Negro voices almost invariably reg-
istered better on the sound strip than those of other
groups.[8]

From the foregoing facts, it is evident that it was
not until 1935 that Negro artists found any success
at Hollywood studios. The screen, for reasons already
pointed out, had shunned the Negro. Negro drama on
the screen had been experimented with since soon
after the close of the Great War, and occasionally
thereafter, but invariably with financial loss. In 1935,

[7] The Washington *Tribune*, December 3, 1937.
[8] *Ibid.*, December 3, 1937.

there came an awakening as to the desirability of showing Negro productions. In that year, James Thompson played in "The Petrified Forest" in the role of Gangster Piles. Also during that year Paul White, a versatile young dancer, went to Hollywood where he was featured in Metro-Goldwyn-Mayer's "Here Comes the Band." Clinton Rosamond played the role of a star in his portrayal of the school janitor in "They Won't Forget."

Richard Huey who had an important role in "Three Men on a Horse," which played to capacity houses on Broadway for two years, was also in the screen version of the picture, produced by Warner Brothers in 1936.

In November, 1937, Edna Mae Harris realized the ambition of her lifetime when she was chosen to play opposite Joe Louis in "The Spirit of Youth," which featured the champion as the master of the prize ring. It is said that Freda Washington declined the role given to Edna Mae Harris because the salary was insufficient.[9] Although it is difficult to determine the merit of the play, or the financial success it had, the consensus of opinion was that Edna Mae Harris, with her personality and stage experience, looms as a moving picture star.

The Negro at the Microphone

Radio programs of the Negro have been less numerous and less popular than any other kind of entertainment. Again, as already observed, the radio attempts to appease a vast audience made up of various elements, who are prospective customers of the article that a particular program advertises. One serial program of interest, however, was the beautiful legend of

[9] *Ibid.*, December 3, 1937.

"John Henry."[10] The program was broadcast Sunday evenings during the winter of 1933. The story was that of a group of persons who gathered around Uncle Sim, the Black River Giant, as the old man recounted one tall tale after the other, concerning strange and unusual happenings along the banks of the powerful Mississippi. The roustabout, John Henry, was characterized by Juano Hernandez. Supporting Hernandez at the microphone were Jack McDowell, Emett Lampkins, the late Rose McClendon, Richard Huey, and Maurice Ellis. In reference to the program, Professor William F. Ogburn of the University of Chicago, wired to the management of the Columbia Broadcasting Company:

"'John Henry' radio drama was a beautiful artistic achievement, growing out of American soil, close to the psychology of the people. It is very suggestive for the future artistic possibilities of the radio."[11]

Still greater radio achievement has been made by the Mills Brothers, who have delighted listeners with their exceptional talent. Their original technique and quality of voice have made a distinct contribution to forms of entertainment.

Orchestras, bands, and music of every description have consumed no small amount of radio time. Since 1930, Cab Calloway and Duke Ellington have been favorites of the radio. Audiences and broadcasting systems have welcomed their talents.

The Negro Actors Guild of America with a brilliant cast of dramatic stars made radio history on June 30, 1930, in a broadcast version of "In Abraham's Bosom." Playing the main role was Frank

[10] Roark Bradford, *John Henry*. New York: Harper and Brothers, 1931, pp. 150-158.
[11] New York *World Telegram*, March 9, 1933.

DRAMA IN MOVING PICTURES AND RADIO

Wilson, who was in the stage production in 1926-1927. Laura Bowman played the role of Abe's querulous mother. Other members of the radio cast were Juano Hernandez, Goldie McAllister, Christolo Williams, Homer Smith and William Edmonson.

Sam Stewart and Slim Gaillard, known as Slim and Slam, are, perhaps, the most popular swing teams on the radio. Playing and singing their composition, "Flat Foot Flugie," in such spectacular fashion, June 4, 1939, on Pat Baron's coast-to-coast program over the Mutual Broadcasting System, they left American jitterbugers gasping.

Having long since gained fame as a producer and arranger, Carlton Moss enhanced his prestige by presenting his dramalogues "Careless Love," "Folks from Dixie" and "Noah" over the National Broadcasting System. His ambition is to broadcast his satire of the filibuster against the anti-lynching bill, which was a highlight of the Negro Cultural Committee of New York.

In the winter of 1938, "Harlem Varieties" came over the air via Station WTNS, every Saturday at eight P. M. The broadcast was handled by Jimmy Christian. "Harlem Varieties" consists of a program of "top notch" colored orchestra recordings. Delightfully done also was "Tales of Harlem," conducted by Joe Bostic, over WMCA, during the same winter. In May of 1938, Mercedes Gilbert starred over the air in "Ma Johnson's Rooming House." She was ably supported by Henrietta Lovelace.

During the winter of 1938-1939, a large number of others made flashes on radio programs. For a while, Bob Howard was with the Glider Shaving program over the National Broadcasting System. Gee Gee James has done a fine job in "Hill Top House." Eddie Gee has appeared in Rudy Vallee's shows. For a time, Hattie Noel was on Eddie Cantor's program. Lionel Hampton and Teddy Wilson added zest to the Benny Goodman's "Camel Caravan." Billy Holliday was a fleeting success on the Old Gold show; on the program was also Artie Shaw. June Richmond thrilled radio listeners on Jimmy Dorsey's broadcasts; besides he was heard regularly with Cab Calloway's orchestra from coast-to-coast. Alberta Hunter made impressive showings in the National Broadcasting System, with a white orchestra. Maxine Sullivan sustained her reputation as the foremost exponent of swing music. In March, 1939, Etta Moten of stage and screen was with "Cabin at the Crossroads," sponsored by Quaker Oats, five times a week. The National Negro Hour emanating from Cleveland was a regular feature of the Columbia Broadcasting network. On June 1, 1939, the Southernaires celebrated the tenth anniversary of the famous quartette's broadcasts over the National Broadcasting System. "Wings Over Jordan," a Cleveland choir, continued its regular Sunday morning broadcasts, with leading educators and professional men and women doing the speaking.

SUMMARY

The Negro in moving pictures, and on radio programs cannot yet assert that he has been successful in either of those fields. The apparent reason has been that southern audiences have failed to appreciate Negro entertainment on radio or screen. Not until 1935 did the Negro show signs of growth and vigor in this phase of drama. Since then he has been making steady progress.

CHAPTER XI

NEGRO DRAMA AND THE FEDERAL THEATRE PROJECT

A nation-wide survey of what the Federal Theatre Unit did among Negroes is not possible or necessary, even did time and space permit. The movement was well under way in the larger cities of the country. Many weak shows have been produced and much time and money expended without commensurate returns. Taken in its broadest outline, however, the unit has warranted its existence, despite the hand of Congress which terminated it in July, 1939.

The dramatic activities of this unit of the W.P.A. have made drama accessible to the general public at very reasonable prices, and, in some instances, without price. Local sponsors have attacked difficult problems in the field of drama, and, to some extent, have worked them out. This project has not only given employment to thousands of amateurs and semi-professionals, but, when the Government took over the responsibility of aiding those in the various arts, this unit gradually raised its standards of production.[1] Sorting out the competents from the incompetents was a difficult task. But insistence on only the fit bore reward.

The Federal Negro Theatre gradually became more balanced and coordinated, and extended its scope of usefulness to include not only actors, as such, but also those who desired to become actors. Instruction

[1] The New York *Times*, October 27, 1937.

in writing, directing, acting and producing was given to both old and young, laymen and semi-professionals. The project afforded abundant opportunities in creative work—opportunities for development through self-criticism, and constructive criticism by experienced playwrights and producers. In other words, the potential actor and playwright had a laboratory in which they could experiment. For instance, the Lafayette Theatre building in Harlem was taken over by the Government and financed largely for such a purpose.

Another praiseworthy feature of the Negro unit lay in the fact, that as actors developed efficiency, they found expression and employment on the legitimate stage.[2] When these amateurs matured into players of experience and finesse, they were sought by managers and producers of the professional stage.

At first there was the question as to whether admissions should be charged to see the productions, and if so, how much. The problem was solved by charging a top price of forty cents for orchestral seats and twenty-five cents for balcony seats.[3]

On February 4, 1936, the Negro division of the New York Federal Theatre Project produced Frank Wilson's latest composition, "Walk Together Chillun." This time Wilson had a message to deliver, but only to the colored race. Writing in simple, direct and apparently sincere terms, he reminds the Negroes that disagreement and lack of solidarity have hampered their progress. The Negro, he thinks, has concerned himself too much with caste and sectional superiority.

[2] The *Afro-American*, January 3, 1938.
[3] The New York *Times*, *op. cit.*

DRAMA AND THE FEDERAL THEATRE

Laying the scene of action in an eastern city, he shows how friction develops when a group of Georgia laborers invade the town. These Georgia workers not only compete with those of the East, but precipitate a race riot. At this stage of development, Wilson demonstrates that he is a dramatic technician, as he subtly plays with these sore spots. It is not difficult to discern that his sympathy lies with the Negroes of the East.

Aside from the spirituals, which should have rest from Negro plays, the playwright shows that the Negro has come North on a fool's errand, and that he has been duped by white men canvassing the South for temporary cheap labor. He lashes the ministry for its indifference and complacency.

Presented at the Lafayette Theatre, ''Walk Together Chillun'' stirred the audience to outbursts of applause. Gus Smith, veteran actor and dabbler in dramatics, demonstrated strength and merit, heading his Georgia delegation. Cliver Foster, as minister, was well aware of his function. Despite the fact that the play has serious breaks and often violates technical principles, it is above the average Negro play in content and dramaturgy.

An interesting play, a sensational offering of the New Jersey W.P.A. Federal Theatre Company at the Maxine Elliott Theatre, stirred up widespread comment because of its theme of inter-racial prejudice. This was ''The Trial of Dr. Beck.'' The bold discussion in the play of color prejudice among Negroes themselves made the effort one of the most controversial of the W.P.A. unit.[4]

---

[4] The Washington *Tribune*, June 16, 1937.

When the play was staged in New Jersey it was supervised by Adele Gutman Nathan and staged by Louis M. Simon. The principal characters were Dorothy Washington and Kenneth Renwick. The latter playing the role of Dr. Beck. The play created such a sensation that the Harlem unit of the W.P.A. produced it with marked success. Whatever creates a sensation appeals to Harlemites.

"The Case of Philip Lawrence," another such piece, had its premiere at the Lafayette Theatre, New York City, June 8, 1937. Burns Mantle of the New York *Daily News* entitled his headline thus:[5]

> "Negro Theatre Stages a Colored Broadway
> With a Mixed Cast in Harlem."

Brooks Atkinson of the New York *Times* began his two-column critique of the production with "Up in Harlem the Negro Unit of the Federal Theatre is making a laudable attempt to stand on its own dramatic feet. 'The Case of Philip Lawrence' exploits the local problems of a race handicapped by constricted social opportunities.'"[6]

Maurice Ellis, who played the role of Philip Lawrence in the New York setting, did well the part of a college graduate who could not get a decent job, but had to accept the job of porter, carrying bags in the Grand Central Terminal. Feeling that he deserves a better position, Philip meets a policy king who makes him master of ceremonies in a night club, in which money is plentiful and opportunity of advancement rapid—in fact, too rapid, for he all but goes to the electric chair on a framed charge of having killed a gangster. George MacEntee (white) showed ability

---

[5] The New York *Daily News*, June 9, 1937.
[6] The New York *Times*, June 9, 1937.

in writing the story, especially those lines which concern the race problem. Augustus Smith, director, on the other hand, was obviously at a disadvantage in attempting to reproduce the night life of Harlem.

Another piece that is a fair representative of W.P.A. creations is "Turpentine," a folk play in three acts, dealing with life among the Florida pines and the struggles of modern workmen. The play was written by Augustus Smith, Negro, and Peter Morrell, of little dramatic background, but who had a desire to reveal what goes on in the Florida pines. In other words, the play concerns itself with the problems of the turpentine industry, and the subsequent "teaming up" of the white and black workers, who are eventually compensated with higher wages and better working conditions. As is true of most proletarian literature, the bosses are vanquished, whereas the underdog gets what he goes after.

While the piece appears to be an honest indictment, it is not a work of excellent art. And though it arrives at the central point and frankly states it, there is, nevertheless, evidence of a lack of ability on the part of Smith and Morrell to put material together properly. Yet, these two men deserve commendation for their effort.

In their development of character, the authors also deserve credit. They chose "Forty-Four" for their hero, who not only had the courage to fight for his inherent rights as well as those of his followers, but who manfully defended the virtue of Negro women. Although his methods and dialogue were at times overdone, he seldom failed to accomplish his purpose. He was vivid and accurate, employing humor and pathos.

The spring and summer of 1936 stand out in accomplishment from all other seasons, in regard to the Unit. Audiences had become disgusted with productions that seemed to them commonplace and ugly and that dealt with the everyday life about them and their southern brothers. Since the New York Negro had culture and appreciation, the question was raised as to why the W.P.A. project did not put on a show of intrinsic merit. There were those who saw nothing informational or ideal in the lives and social activities of persons about them.

Hence, on April 13, 1936, at the Lafayette Theatre, New York City, the premiere of a different type of production, a Haitian Macbeth, was presented. The play proved to be a success. The presence of Broadway, Fifth Avenue and Park Avenue play lovers added to the multitude that thronged the theatre.

The scenery and artistry of the play were all that could be desired. Edna Thomas in her portrayal of the heroine interpreted her role well. The casting of Jack Carter in the leading role showed rare insight. His splendid portrayals in ''Porgy'' and ''Stevedore'' were good, to be sure, but in neither of those did he emerge with more credit than he did in Shakespeare's immortal tragedy.

So successful was the production in Harlem that it was taken to the Adelphi Theatre on 58th Street, where it played to appreciative audiences for four weeks, before going on a successful tour, and winding up at the Texas Centennial in the summer of 1936.

One of the latest efforts of the Negro W.P.A. Unit was the production of three of Eugene O'Neill's one-act plays, ''Moon of the Caribbean,'' ''Bound East for Cardiff,'' and ''The Long Voyage Home,'' presented at the Lafayette Theatre in New York in December,

1937. Running true to his tradition, O'Neill presents no long drawn out preachments in these recent offerings.

Even though these particular plays are difficult to produce and act, the Unit has surmounted, seemingly, insuperable obstacles. Profiting from experience, the actors played their roles with seriousness, and displayed a degree of finesse in their acting.

The plots and themes of the plays deal with situations and backgrounds similar to the days preceding and including the World War. "Moon of the Caribbean" is entirely devoid of plot. Nevertheless, it serves as an introduction of the other plays.

The best characterization was decidedly in favor of Jacqueline Martin, who did a good performance in "The Long Voyage Home." Wardell Saunders and Lionel Monagas deserve commendation for their fine interpretations of difficult lines.

About this time, too, William Du Bois, a newspaper man by vocation and a playwright by avocation, was going from producer to producer trying to get his script accepted. Finally, the New York Federal Theatre decided to present his play, and on March 2, 1938, the Harlem W.P.A. Project raised the curtain on the first legitimate production of "Haiti."

On March 9, one week after the premiere, the Shubert Theatre made overtures to the Federal Theatre Project with the idea of launching the play at the Forty-sixth Street Theatre. Archie Hill, one of the sponsors of the local project, advised the Shubert officials that such a plan was not feasible. The general excitement over the production, however, caused the local officials to install the play in Daly's Theatre, Sixty-third Street, east of Broadway.

THE NEGRO AND THE DRAMA

Using the bloody records of the Haitian insurrection of 1802, William Du Bois has dramatized a good version of an old regime. The Federal Theatre assisted him with an expensively fine set. Hence, "Haiti" had two months of gusty performances. The author has followed history rather closely, for he opens his first act with Napoleon landing troops in Haiti to suppress a rebellion. Inspired by Toussaint Louverture and Christophe, the Negroes go from the hills and slaughter the French.

Gleaming with stage bearing and determination, Rex Ingram played Christophe with demonstrated deeds of courage. Assisting Ingram with considerable finesse were Alvin Childress and Louis Sharp. Lovers of battle and excitement were highly entertained with this butchering melodrama. Few if any like to see human beings butchered. But those who are familiar with the history of the oppressed cannot help admiring those brave Haitians who defended their shores. From the point of view of psychology, theme and action "Haiti" is the best show to date dealing with a Negro plot.

In another production the New York Federal Theatre Project allowed the philosophy of George Bernard Shaw to express the thoughts of the oppressed minorities of the world. The persecution of Christians of Roman times is comparable to the persecutions of the modern Negro. Shaw has perennially preached for those who have been pushed to the lowest level of society. In so doing he satirizes those who are responsible, and accordingly makes out a good case against the guilty in "Androcles and the Lion."

This production, in a prologue and two acts, was presented in March, 1938, at the Lafayette Theatre,

New York. Daniel Haynes, who made theatrical history as the leading character in "Halleluiah," represented all of the earmarks of a race tortured with sorrows. Singing "I Am Bound for the Promised Land," Haynes embodied the earnestness and emotions of Ferrovius, flawlessly. The Lion was well portrayed by A. Bates. Arthur Wilson did the movements and lines of Androcles smoothly and effectively. With a mixture of dramatic ingredients, Edna Thomas was an almost perfect Lavinia. Following close behind "Haiti," it was nearly as successful. If it were weaker in action it compensated in the rich voice of Daniel Haynes. None would question that the venerable Shaw wrote a good play. Were it not for the poor diction of some of the actors few would criticise the production as a whole.

A three-act comedy of Negro life, "Mississippi Rainbow" opened in March, 1939, at the Forty-ninth Street Theatre, New York City. The story is that of Henry Washington who quits physical labor to give his brain a chance to work for him. Meanwhile, his wife and son toil to support the family. The son sacrifices an opportunity to get a musical education. But alas, as everybody loses confidence in Washington's schemes, and denounces him as a lazy tramp, his idea materializes. The wife no longer works. Charles marries the girl he has seduced and takes the wife and child to New York, where he studies music. In theme and plot "Mississippi Rainbow" is weak. The story is too old to be refreshing, and the author has not assiduously attended to details.

Based on the original variation of the Gilbert and Sullivan opera, "Mikado" is the "Swing Mikado," which was first produced by the Federal Project of

Chicago. Purchased by private industry of New York, the show came to Broadway, where it had a flash. But the "Hot Mikado" which had a superior cast offered too much competition, and the New York engagement soon came to an end. Although the cast disbanded, the principal characters, including the management, went to California, where they organized a group of local talent, and set up under the supervision of the Federal Theatre Project.

In July, 1939, Hall Johnson's latest version of "Run Little Chillun" was given a rumbling hand in Los Angeles. The folk drama opened there July 22, at the Mayan Theatre, under the supervision of the W.P.A. Theatre and Music Project.

SUMMARY

It is not surprising to find that the sincere and unpretentious efforts of actors and playwrights in the Federal Theatre Unit were temporary. Their work was not particularly impressive or skillful from the point of view of dramatic art. Most of these plays were hardly more than the setting forth of social problems—that is, if one judges them in terms of art. On the other hand, Federal Theatre Unit has served a worthwhile purpose. First of all, it has given employment. Second, it has put dramatic entertainment within the reach of the average individual. Third, it has served as a laboratory for those with a creative urge.

CHAPTER XII

INCIDENTAL DRAMA

Among other works will be found those with vary-
ing merit. A few of this group of plays have been
produced by professionals; some have been produced
by amateurs, while there is no record of the production of others. Some of them are by neither white
nor black authors and producers, but by whites who
have attempted to burlesque black themes, and some
by Negroes dealing with Negro themes. Still others
have Negro themes, *with the remaining part of the
play white.*

LIGHT COMEDY

As light comedy, Michael Gold, author of "Hoboken
Blues," has attempted to dramatize the plight of a
nonchalant, shiftless, easy-going, banjo-playing Negro of Harlem. Assuming that such a person will re-
spond to religious preachment, Gold places him in a
revival meeting, with the idea of scaring him into getting a job. This method failing, the banjo player is
severely beaten over the head with a Hoboken police-
man's night stick. Interwoven into this thin story is
a series of mediocre songs and dances, together with
an abundance of trite dialogue. Hence, the play is
without intrinsic value.

The action of "Brown Buddies," another such
piece, begins in an East St. Louis shanty, rapidly ex-
tending across the sea to war zones, and back again to

East St. Louis. Surrounded by war and its attendant misery, the actors perform lustrous deeds. However, on Armistice Day the war clouds are lifted, and everybody is happy. At this stage of events national prohibition goes into effect, but not before the antics of two of the comedians.

For the most part, "Brown Buddies" is a show of dancing and singing. Incidentally, when it was produced in New York City in October, 1930, Bill Robinson and Adelaide Hall were in the main roles. And again, though crippled by a stray bullet of a Pittsburgh officer, Robinson displayed a sense of rhythmic tempo that was to the satisfaction of New York's theatre set. Adelaide Hall made a sensational hit with the singing of "Give Me a Man Like That." It is said that John Mason added color and mirth to the occasion with his comic monologue. Pike Davis and his "Brown Buddies" orchestra, playing "Happy" and "When a Black Man's Blue," aided in the merriment. Of Ada Brown, John Mason Brown of the New York *Evening Post* said, "As an evening's entertainment 'Brown Buddies' gains considerably because of the elephantine vitality of Ada Brown, who is four side-shows all in one." Though brightened by rare Negro songs and dance, "Brown Buddies" is nothing more than a series of light, refreshing episodes.

"Old Man Satan," somewhat like "The Green Pastures," deals with the Negro's conception of the rise and fall of Satan, and the mental state of a mammy, who has apparitions of Satan and the hereafter. The play was written and produced in New York by Donald Heywood, a West Indian Negro. It is thought by Hayes Pryor, who played in the 1930 production of it, that because of irregular management the play failed. Though a one-act play, it was full of good dancing, singing and clever antics. Moreover, it was made all the more lively by the fine acting of the "cream" of colored entertainment. An audience may expect more than mere drollery from a cast in which Georgette Harvey, Edna Thomas and Mike Jackson appear. They were ably assisted by Phyllis Hunt, A. B. Comathiere, Dan Michael and Lionel Monagas.

"Hell's Alley," written by Alvin Childress and Alice Herndon, was produced by the Lafayette Players of New York. The scene of action takes place in an alley, in which a gangster carries on his trade of swindling and victimizing unsuspecting persons who pass. The main character, who is a shrewd gambler, often finds it expedient to send one of his henchmen out to track down "new suckers." Such a plot is not only old and trite, but presents a bad moral. Besides, it is not good sociology. With all of their experience and finesse, not even the delightful acting of Hayes Pryor, Alice Herndon, Tom Moseley, Laura Brown, Billy Sheppard and A. B. Comathiere were able to lift it above the level of mediocrity.

"Memory Lane" was a series of skits in memory of the outstanding actors of the gay nineties, presented in Detroit, Michigan, November 20, 1933. Each of this collection of rare talent performed in the category of his specialty. For instance, W. C. Handy played his Blues on the cornet. J. Rosamond Johnson, best known for the music he set to "Lift Every Voice and Sing" and the composition of many of the songs sung by the late Bert Williams, played his "Lazy Moon" and others of his popular hits.

In "Potee's Gal" the hero has a series of ups-and-downs in the pursuance of the girl of his heart. In

177

this satire Edward C. L. Adams attempts to poke fun at a group of Negroes in Columbia, South Carolina, whose scene of action shifts from dance hall to church and conversely. The play has ludicrous moments when Potee's girl is observed in the embrace of another man, inciting Potee to use his knife rather carelessly. Since it is generally known what the white man thinks of Negro life, this play reveals no sterling qualities.

In "The Second Coming" George Bryant has given his impression of southern Negroes' hilarity as it is merged with their conception of life after death. Though not a play of distinctive merit, it was sufficiently funny to arouse the interest of many who saw it at the Provincetown Play House, New York City, when it was produced there in 1931. In the title role, A. B. Comathiere apparently pleased the critics and the audience. Hayes Pryor, Lloyd Russell and Irving Hopkins also received the critics' praise.

"The Marriage of Cana" is hardly more than a stereotyped comedy of Negro life, exaggerated to the point of melodrama. When it was produced at the Plymouth Theatre, New York City, entertaining moments were made largely by a well rehearsed cast. The performance of Juano Hernandez, Alice Ramsey, Hayes Pryor and James E. Owens was considered superb.

Saturated with comedy, satire and pathos, "Blue and the Gray" attempts to give the social side of army life. It does not rise to the level of a great production.

Harlem theatregoers were highly entertained when they attended Kenyon Nicholson's version of "Sailor Beware." Presented during the winter of 1934, this singing-dancing play had no plot and needed none, for when Carrington Lewis, Paul Johnson, James Dunmore, Juanita Hall, Ken Renard, Dorothy Lincoln and Christola Williams appear on the stage, comic entertainment becomes the order of the occasion.

"Great Day," presented in October, 1929, at the Cosmopolitan Theatre, New York City, is both an operetta and a comedy and at the same time neither. For instance, the famous Miller and Lyle were present with all their fun making. It is said that they were especially amusing in their mispronunciation of polysyllables. They were in other ways delightful in their interludes between the songs. And, too, any show of Negroes known as the Jubilee Ensemble is a rare treat. An exceptional attraction was the splendid baritone of Lois Deppe. Time and again the cast halted the show, as the audience demanded encores of "Without a Song," and "Great Day."

In this connection the Silas Green Theatrical Company deserves attention. It is still a major attraction after 51 years of traveling up and down and across the country. Known as "Silas Green from New Orleans," it is the oldest Negro road show in the United States. Organized in 1888 by the Whitney Brothers, this comic institution has been on the road ever since. At the time of its organization the featured attractions were the antics of horses, trained by Professor Ephe Williams. For a while, Williams' aid caused him to become co-owner. When the tent and properties of the show were destroyed in 1907, the Whitneys decided to withdraw their support. They were persuaded, however, by R. C. Puggsley, of the Puggsley Brothers Quartette, to take what was left of the original show on a "barn-storming" tour. Gradual

179

improvements were made in all departments until its present size and value were attained.

In 1921, Williams sold out to Charles Collier, present owner, who has successfully carried on in traditional form. During its half century of existence, the show has had but four Silas Greens. Eddie Stafford was the first comedian to make Silas Green a by-word. He was followed by Leroy Knox, Ford Wiggins, and Happy Hampton. Gaines, the producer, became affiliated with the show in 1913, when he and his brother displayed their acrobatic ability. Gaines left ''Silas Green'' to play Keith's vaudeville circuit. Subsequently, he and his brother were in the finale of Warner Brothers' ''Gold Diggers of Broadway.'' He rejoined ''Silas Green'' in 1931 as producer. No one who has seen ''Silas Green from New Orleans'' will deny that it is a good show. It is far superior to much one sees on Broadway. ''Silas Green'' is a finished production and pictorially effective.

Here we should mention also some other reviews. Casual perusal of Burns Mantle's ''Best Plays'' immediately indicates that Negro fantasies have been rapidly parading before Broadway theatre-goers ever since ''Shuffle Along'' and ''Running Wild'' made their breath-taking appearances. The plays that followed, however, made a flash, flickered and died as suddenly as they had appeared. Like Lew Leslie's ''Black Birds'' that has taken a trip to Broadway annually for the last twelve years, these shows of song, dance and comic drollery were hardly more than repetitious caricature of Negro hilarity. Meanwhile, it was noted, though, that this talent was well rehearsed and wore beautifully designed costumes.

Among the better of this class of productions that

played to Broadway audiences were: "Dixie to Broadway" (1925), "Lucky Sambo" (1925), "My Magnolia" (1926), "Hot Chocolates" (1929), "Change Your Luck" (1930), "Africana" (1927), "Deep Harlem" (1926), "Sugar Hill" (1931), "Rhapsody in Black" (1931), "Black Rhythm" (1936). Though these shows were not long to live among the keen competition on Broadway, they included in their casts the best talent in Negro theatrical circles. The Tutt Brothers, Bill Robinson, Ethel Waters, Adelaide Hall and countless other Harlem entertainers were there to help put the show "across the footlights." In the early 1920's Florence Mills was a top-ranking star whose rich, musical voice was often sought.

The popularity of Florence Mills was greatest between 1914 and 1927. She was born January 25, 1895. She made her first dramatic appearance at the age of four in the Bijou Theatre in Washington, D. C. Soon after that she had small roles in other plays. In 1914 she became associated with Buddy Gilmore with whom she toured the East and West, singing and dancing in night clubs. Her husband, U. S. Thompson, said that "she was the first colored woman to headline at Keith's Palace."

In 1926 she was the star in Lew Leslie's "Black Birds." After a year's run in America, Leslie took the cast to Paris for an engagement of four weeks, which was extended to sixteen weeks because of the popularity of the play. Then the troupe went to London, where, it is said, the Prince of Wales saw its performance twenty times.

"Come Along Mandy," a farce-comedy in two acts, was produced at the Park Theatre, New York City, beginning September 13, 1917. It is thought that the war which at that time was being waged against imperial Germany prevented a longer than three-day run of the play. A lively and good natured burlesque, and any one looking for more amusing, rattle-brained jesting would have difficulty. A clean story, fast action, and an abundance of comedy, "Come Along Mandy" is gay and entertaining. Featured in the performance were two stage favorites, Salem Tutt Whitney and J. Homer Tutt. Others in the production were Edna Gibbs, Anna Scroggins, Harold Marshall, Irene Lander, Joseph Purnell and Charles Hawkins.

"Little Black Sambo and the Tigers," a comedy fantasy in three acts, by Charlotte Chorpenning, was first produced at the Goodman Theatre, Chicago, and was later used by various Junior League theatres. A new and original play, the charm and effectiveness of it consist in the amusing story and the combination of comedy, character and a sort of jungle poetry, full of suggestion and color. Sambo, who is a sensitive and wistful African dreamer, has a sense of rhythm in his body and speech. It is a quick moving play that has no axe to grind and, though light, this comedy is romantic and exuberant.

In 1919 appeared "Rackey," in some respects a piece which was garnished melodrama like Randolph Edmonds' "Bad Man." Combining comedy with realism, Ernest Culbertson here deals with a criminal who has repented. The piece is sketchy and disjointed.

Recent Problem Drama

The plot of "White Man" is the vexatious situation in which a light skinned Negro finds himself after marriage to a white girl. His presence is cherished neither by the whites nor by the blacks. Just before the baby's birth, he reveals his identity to his wife, who says it does not matter. Samson Raphaelson, author of the play, seems to think that it does. In fact, he knows that it mattered to her father, who forces her to abandon her husband and child.

As serious drama, "White Man" made little impression on the audiences that saw it in October, 1930; at least their snickers indicated as much. Since the first aim of drama is to entertain, it is not assumed that "White Man" has all of the qualifications of good drama.

"Potter's Field," produced by a professional company in April, 1934, was warmly received though closed after a short run. After much revision and cutting the piece was revived on the New York stage as "Roll, Sweet Chariot." One of the most impressive scenes in the play is the one in which a group of convicts are forced to work on a road that runs through their former neighborhood. To the delight of white audiences and readers they are naturally embarrassed on seeing their friends snigger at their plight. The entire play is designed to show what the white man thinks of Negro life and character. The author has reached down into the slums for its sordid life and animal nature. The Negro's shiftlessness and disregard for the future also come within the author's purview. Although New York producers hung a show on this theme, it does not have a refreshing plot. "Roll, Sweet Chariot" is so stale that it approaches burlesque.

Those who like prison melodrama cannot prevent admiring Frederick Schlick's "Bloodstream," a play

of revolting convicts. With the scene of action laid
in a coal mine, whites and blacks combine their force
to repulse the brutal treatment of their employers.
Four of the revolters are Negroes. In 1932, when the
play was produced in New York the roles of Negroes
were portrayed by William Andrews, Ernest R. Whitman, Wayland Rudd, and Frank Wilson, who as usual
was firm. Critics were of the opinion that they acted
simply and forcefully, inspiring with propriety a play
that was both repelling and engaging to many that
saw it.

In "Mighty Wind a'Blowin'," Alice Holdship
Ware has laid the scene in Ben's Shanty, on a cotton
plantation in Arkansas. She attempts to recite the
story of a Negro share-cropper, Ben, and the exploitation of his family, by a plantation owner. In this
drama of stark realism, the share-croppers have no
recourse but to yield to the cruel whims of Grimstead,
who threatens to turn his victims over to the sheriff,
"who is asettin on mah front po'ch playin' cyards."
That the author has treated a subject which is familiar to thousands of tenant farmers of the South, no
one dares to question, but American lovers of the
theatre care not to have the sins of their brothers flash
back in the form of entertainment. Consequently,
when the play was produced by the New Theatre
League of New York, it was too raw to be widely es-
teemed, and closed forthwith. Since, however, the
theme has depth, and has not been over-worked, and
is put together with a degree of dramatic technique,
admirers of proletarian drama may find in it spots of
refreshing moments.

"Hand of Fate," or "Fifty Years After," by
Beresford Gale, like "Mighty Wind a-Blowin'," also

has its setting on a cotton plantation. Choosing Virginia for his place of action, the author has Richard Walker for his hero. Upon reaching maturity, Richard assumes that conditions of the South are unbearable, and accordingly decides to migrate to the North. The day before his scheduled departure, the master of the plantation comes upon the scene, and plots the destruction of Richard's intentions. The master's machinations are frustrated, however, by another white man, who is a friend of the Negro. The heroine of the play and sweetheart of Walker, defies death, and by strategic deeds helps her lover to escape.

This story does not present a real chronicle of life, for it is more idealistic than realistic. Only in fiction could Richard have hardly realized the aid of this particular white man. When good luck smiles upon Richard, he returns to the scene, only again to be thwarted by Craven, the master. But this time the cards are stacked against Craven, and for reasons unexplained Craven is sent to jail. Justice having triumphed, Richard makes good and marries the girl of his youth. Written from a Negro's point of view, the play is only a beautiful dream. Thus, it is one of those situations often desired but never quite attained. As serious drama, it is too unreal to be of much benefit. People are inclined to favor drama that is a reproduction of the situation of life, slightly colored.

"A Million Black and White Are Saying No" is similar in theme to "Angelo Herndon," which strongly turns the searchlights on a Georgia chain gang. Based on the imprisonment of Angelo Herndon, a young Negro Communist, the play set out to show that Herndon was condemned not because of any violation of statute, but because of his attempt to organize white and black workers of Georgia. Produced as propaganda by the New Theatre League of New York, these plays demand the unconditional release of Herndon.

"The Noose," "Big Show," "Judge Lynch," "White Heat," "Black Belt," "The Tree," "Lawd Does You Understand?" and "Sweet Land" are plays, the themes of which embrace the South's mob law method of handling fractious Negroes. Of these, "The Tree" seems to have been more successful as stage material, for it was presented for a week at the Park Lane Theatre, New York City, beginning April 12, 1932. Idealistic in theme, it features a white man, who, out of remorse, prefers to die than to live knowing he is guilty of a crime for which a Negro was lynched. Despite the fact that it is a ringing indictment of mobs that take the law into their hands, it could not thrive even on liberal Broadway. The very intensity of its indictment was the reason for its short sojourn. Seekers of entertainment are not looking for such rank stench.

John W. Rogers' "Judge Lynch," which is fairly dramatized, has white characters, three of whom have lynched a Negro for a crime he did not commit. After the lynching, overwhelming evidence supports his innocence, yet not the slightest degree of chagrin is apparent. In "White Heat" and "Big Blow" lynchings are thwarted because the cowards suddenly become conscious-stricken. The heroine of "The Noose" finds consolation in the fact that her relative has attempted to prevent the lynchings of a Negro accused of rape, only to become stunned to learn that her own husband has tied the rope around the victim's neck. "Lawd, Does You Understand?" has an unusual departure from the average play written on the lynch subject. Rather than let her grandson be lynched by a bloodthirsty mob, Aunt Doady feeds him hemlock. Because the play is designed as a weapon against lynching, the Association of Southern Women for the Prevention of Lynching awarded its author, Ann Seymour, a medal. When the play was presented at Paine College, Augusta, Georgia, in December, 1936, it was warmly received.

Other plays of the lynch evil need not be discussed here, as they are less artless than these and add nothing new to an overworked theme. Unlike the author of "Never No More," the writers of these plays indicate that they are lacking in the basic mechanics of histrionic foundation. They seem to feel that they have been destined both by God and man to rid society of the disaster, but they have failed to prepare themselves for the task. Hence, the plays are weak, formless, plotless and without friction. A play, in some respects, is like a debate, in that if one side is overwhelmingly stronger than the other side, very little interest is manifested. Audiences like to see evenly opposing forces, a clash, a balanced situation. This drama does not possess these assets, and accordingly, it has not been widely heard.

Others of a different theme are not of a higher level. Israel Du Bois' "Blood of Kings" is of importance merely because it is classified as a play. Like many other mulattoes, the main character, Duane, attempts to cross the color line. The assumption here rests upon a double claim. In the first place, notwithstanding a few drops of colored blood, Duane believes he is actually white. In the second place, he reasons that he has royal blood in his veins. Obsessed with this two-fold conviction, he forces his way into white gatherings. Ofttimes he is successful, only to be observed at other times by those who know "a damn nigger" anywhere they see him. Had Duane argued on the grounds of civil rights, the play would have a greater claim to be heard. But lacking in approach and technical details, the play fails to drive home a social message.

Departing from her trashy "Scarlet Sister Mary," Julia Peterkin, who lays the scene of her fictions in South Carolina, stresses better race relations in "Boy-Chillun." Based on a segregation note, also, is "Like a Flame," by Alice Holdship Ware, whose claim as a dramatist rests heavily upon "Mighty Wind a-Blowin'." "Like a Flame," a dramatized version of Langston Hughes' "Tomorrow," deals with Hughes' observations of French night clubs, in which American tourists attempt to draw the color line.

Saturated with voodooism, charms, witchcraft and superstition are "Falling of the Moon," "Zombi," "Come Seven" and "Quagmire." These small dramatic attempts boast of no worth while themes and have none. The customs and magic rites on which these themes are based still prevail in southern parts of the United States. Plays of such character are too naive and trite to receive much notice. Only in rare instances have they enjoyed a measure of success. Since drama loving people are awakening to the desirability of improving their productions, such rubbish is consistently falling into desuetude.

In an attempt that lacks histrionic merit, Georgia Johnson has dramatized a few achievements of Frederick Douglass in a plotless sketch bearing his name. The effort was doubtless sincere but suggests that the author was unaware of stagecraft. The unselfish ambition hardly did justice to the Negro abolitionist. Likewise, ''The Star of Ethiopia'' by the esoteric William E. B. Du Bois possesses few earmarks of sound dramaturgy. An endeavor to parade the accomplishments of 10,000 years before an audience in a single short performance is too much strain on the imagination. Only a director of intensive training and experience would be capable of giving a satisfactory production of it. So did Edward McCoo fail as dramatist in ''Ethiopia at the Bar of Justice'' and Leslie P. Hill in ''Jethro.'' Dr. Hill's ''Jethro'' has aroused some interest, however, if for no other reason than that it was presented at the school over which he presides.

''Family Affairs'' by Frederick W. Bond is simply an attempt to tell the story of a family that has become victimized by the depression. Unable to find employment, Henry, the chief character, is reduced to humiliating distress. The situation is all the more desperate when his wife becomes fretful on finding that the family has to sleep and eat in the same room. Added to this plight is the fact that relatives make their visits frequent and long.

Abram Hill's ''Hell's Half Acre'' has not been presented professionally. The dramatization of the intricate forces at odds in a small, southern town when four persons accused of murder are finally brought to trial, is good, dramatic material. The murderers are found guilty of inciting violence, and sentenced accordingly. If some of the oratory of the piece were eliminated and the technique improved, ''Hell's Half Acre'' would be a good play.

Angelina Grimké's ''Rachel'' discusses the torments

and agony of a girl whose father has been lynched. Lacking in the fundamental principles of drama the piece is preposterous, and will hardly meet the approval of an audience. Again, with the aim of commercializing at the expense of the Harlem Negro, Eulalie Spence has written "Undertow" and "The Starter." Her first hand acquaintance with the New York Negro has resulted in drama of some significance, however slight that significance may be.

Du Bose Heyward departed materially from "Porgy" and "Mamba's Daughter" when he wrote "Brass Ankle." With its setting in his native South Carolina, Heyward has here injected the Mendelian Law. Born to a white couple is a child with Negro-Indian features, the result of ancestral lineage. In the wife's dilemma, she accuses the Negro servant of being the father, whereupon the husband slays her. The narrtive effectively reveals racial prejudice in the raw, when the tragedy occurs.

Earl Aubrey Jones's "Port of No Where," thought to be a winner of acclaim if ever produced, has its setting in a western town near a railroad station where there is a boarding house in which reside prostitutes and railroad hands. With the exception of a light love affair, the remainder of the play deals with murder and all of its terrible aspects.

Turning from his successful "Mulatto" which deals with miscegenation, and two comedies, "Little Ham" and "When the Jack Hollers," the prolific pen of Langston Hughes wrote "Troubled Island," "Scottsboro Limited," "Angelo Herndon Jones" and "Don't You Want to Be Free?" (1939). The last like the preceding three is a significant proletarian drama. Startling in its realism, the play plunges the Negro fresh from his native Africa into the wretched slavery of America; depicts his method of throwing off the shackles of slavery in the solace of his "Go Down Moses." Ending with a Communistic tinge, the play comes to a melodramatic climax with the union of white and black labor, as the following lines suggest, "White worker, here is my hand. Let's get together, folks, and fight, fight, fight!" A bit too stark for professional producers, nevertheless, under the direction of the Suitcase Theatre group, the play ran for several weeks in Harlem.

Paul Peters, who collaborated with George Sklar when he wrote "Stevedore," attempts with little success to reproduce a lynching scene in "Bivouac." Bernice Harris draws upon the time-worn theme of farm tenancy in her "His Jewel." There is nothing exciting or beneficial about this antiquated theme. The same impression may be had of John Remassa's "Mess of Pottage" and Harold Anderson's "Smell the Sweet Savior." Hardly has Herbert Kline helped the theatre with his new version of "John Henry," which urges the union of black and white labor. George Towns' "Sharecropper," which strikes a dynamic blow at the exploitation of tenant farmers, has failed to register on the stage.

"Goat Alley," a hodge-podge of Negro life of the slums of the District of Columbia, adds little information and less technique to the field of drama. Its merit rests upon its fearless attacks upon certain sociological problems of the Negro. One of these problems deals with a girl who remains faithful to the man she loves despite forces operating against such fidelity. Immediately failing as a production of magnitude in 1921, it was revived in 1927 and presented

THE NEGRO AND THE DRAMA

at the Princess Theatre. In its later version it was better appreciated, if for no other reason than that Evelyn Ellis, Louis Johnson and A. B. Comathiere gave excellent interpretation of their lines. The poolroom shiek, Baron Byron, was full of mirth and dressed in splendid attire. Able assistance was given the cast by Dorothy Paul and Jack Carter.

"Police Systems," however, is a gripping picture of the scenes taken from the everyday life of Harlem. The story deals with the law and its agents, with the idea of cleaning up vice and crime. In so doing jail sentences and night sticks are used to advantage. Produced in 1929 at the Alhambra Theatre, the show was not to the liking of a Harlem crammed with similar street scenes. To many a Harlemite, it was a satire of his mischief and moral depravity. Apparently written in haste, "Police System" embraces little that is commendable.

"The Problem of Race," or "The Slave" as does "Fifty Years of Freedom" (1910) deals with the Negro's reaction to new opportunity. Aside from its racial tinge, "The Problem of Race" concerns itself with a man who comes to realize that there is a cultural difference between him and wife. "Fifty Years of Freedom" discusses the development of a Negro, who goes from a cabin to Congress. In their rise to fame the heroes of both plays encounter the problems of domestic work, landlords and adjustment to new environments. Both are sympathetic appreciations of Negro culture, backgrounds and ambitions. "America Grows Up" likewise deals with adjustment of the Negro to his new environment. During the gilded 1920's, the northern man needed labor; thus with flattering salaries, he enticed the Negro to leave the South, only to forsake him stranded when the 1929 depression set in.

As a teacher in Florida, John Matheus was an observer of this migration. He saw officers arrest Negroes when they purchased their railroad tickets. Thinking that such material could be dramatized, he wrote "Cruiter," a study of the conflict between the old and the new Negro at the time of the northern migration during and immediately after the World's War. The Negro had gone to war and returned home when he found conditions worse than before he left. Assuming that the Negro had received a raw deal, Ransom Rideout satirized the situation in "Goin' Home." He fearlessly shows how the Negro fought in France. For a number of years, it has been apparent that the Negro has been worried over his predicament. His reaction to this oppression and exploitation was dramatized in "How Come Lawd," presented by the Negro Guild Theatre of New York, October 1, 1937. Despite the appearance of Rex Ingram in the title role, ably assisted by J. Homer Tutt, the play was weak and without many arresting qualities.

SUMMARY

Plays of this chapter have not blown off rafters, but they are with us and are asking to be considered. Some of them have challenged the attention of amateurs and professionals, whether they have presented these or not. They suggest that theatre folk are continually manifesting zestful enthusiasm both in writing and producing drama. Drama of Negro theme is demanding recognition as a specific theatrical type; these plays need not offer any apology. They are not merely a tour de force mechanically thrown together. Instead several of them have theme, plot, style, and technique. Some are, of course, soaked with propaganda without delicate finesse. In their attempt to throw a strong flashlight on the evils that have infested the race, careless playwrights have destroyed the merit of otherwise good plays.

SUMMARY AND CONCLUSIONS

A. SUMMARY

Since the aims of the writer have been to ascertain what have been the conditions responsible for Negro drama, and what part the Negro has played in the creation of drama, a definite course of procedure was followed. That procedure was: (1) a study of the Negro's background dealing with his innate poetry and song; and (2) a study of dramatic literature dealing with Negro drama, with the underlying conditions responsible. The study has been limited to the dramatic development of the American Negro.

As early as 1820 the Negro began to manifest interest in the theatre, since in 1821, the African Players were making commendable showings in New York City. Immediately after these ventures Ira Aldridge entered the theatre as a handy man, and by the middle of the nineteenth century he was a successful actor, receiving the attention of critics and play-lovers. Victor Sejour, a Louisiana Creole, moved to Paris about the same time and distinguished himself as a playwright.

Beginning in a small way, on southern plantations, minstrelsy was soon to become the distinct form of Negro entertainment. For it was on plantations and in barrooms that the whites first took an interest in the Negro art. It started in the early part of the nineteenth century and continued until the close thereof. At the dawn of the twentieth century, a definite break with the minstrel tradition took place. That break was an improvement in Negro entertainment. Interested in popular songs and light comedy, James Weldon Johnson, Rosamond Johnson, Robert Cole and others wrote for the New York stage from 1895 to 1905. Their aim was to get away from the "coon songs" and black-faced comedy. Meanwhile, segregation and better economic conditions had caused Negroes of the larger cities of the country to build theatres of their own. Moreover, Negro actors interested in musical comedy gradually became numerous. The most colorful of these actors between 1900 and 1910 were Sam Jack, John W. Isham, Bert Williams and George Walker.

The first important compositions based on the Negro, were Ridgley Torrence's three plays, produced in 1917 by Mrs. Emily Hapgood. After the World War, plays were written by such Negroes as Frank Wilson, Miller and Lyle, Hall Johnson, Willis Richardson, Dennis Donoghue, and Langston Hughes. These Negro playwrights made promising beginnings, but, with the exceptions of Langston Hughes and Hall Johnson, interest in their productions rapidly died out. Frank Wilson wrote an extremely promising play in "Meek Mose," but his two other full-length plays achieved but slight distinction.

In 1918 the Provincetown Players of New York put on a program of one-act plays by Eugene O'Neill dealing with Negro themes. "The Emperor Jones," O'Neill's first full-length Negro play, was produced in 1920 with Charles Gilpin in the title-role. After the success of this venture, O'Neill set to work in earnest on Negro themes. Accordingly, in 1924, his "All God's Chillun Got Wings" was produced.

196

SUMMARY AND CONCLUSIONS

O'Neill's interest in Negro themes was the beginning
of a period of unprecedented activity in Negro productions. Experimental writers, thereupon, began to
delve seriously into Negro life and character. The
most notable figure between O'Neill and Connelly was
Paul Green.

Green, a professor at the University of North Carolina, became intimately acquainted with the material
that he was later to use so effectively in "White
Dresses," "In Abraham's Bosom," and "The No
'Count Boy." Many other writers of Negro drama
since 1918, have momentarily made a flash, only to
flicker out as suddenly as they appeared. Marcus Connelly wrote an extremely good play in "Green Pastures" (1929), but his play that followed this first
success has not achieved any distinction.

John Wexley in "They Shall Not Die" (1933), and
Sklar and Peters in "Stevedore" (1934) gave a realistic interpretation of justice accorded Negroes in
southern courts. DuBose and Dorothy Heyward's
"Porgy" is very different from the drama of other
playwrights, yet, it is of distinctly southern life. With
few scattered exceptions, most of the white writers
have been concerned with superficial aspects of Harlem life. Occasionally, playwrights have risen above
the limitations of locale, and written a genuinely significant piece of drama. Such advancement has been
attained by David Belasco in his "Lula Belle" (1926),
Lew Leslie's "Black Birds of 1929," the production
that caused Avis Andrews to receive the acclaim of
theatre people and Mrs. Annie Nathan's "Black
Souls" (1932). Some of the local color sketches are
interesting in their delineation of local characteristics
of speech and environment. Yet, it is undeniable that

most of the playwrights are more interested in the commercial phase than they are in any other possible motive.

Moving picture and radio officials have considered it dangerous to experiment to any appreciable extent with Negro talent. The obvious reason, in either industry, has been that these officials and sponsors of radio programs have attempted to give the audiences the kind of entertainment they have desired. Patrons in certain sections of the country hav been more or less averse to entertainment of Negroes that has not been of the caricature or burlesque variety.

A subject that has received notice in the present work is that of the development of the dance, and the influence that the Negro has had on this development. In earlier days, the American dance was formal, and it was not until the Negro began to introduce dances that this formalism faded out. Since 1920, the public has recognized that the Negro is not only a natural dancer, but a creator of dances. A distinct loss to the art of dancing was the type exemplified by the late Florence Mills. The best known character in the field of dancing since 1920 has been Bill Robinson, whose chief contribution is his highly artistic performance with so little exertion.

The Federal theatre movement among Negroes has not been without merit. The movement has served a two-fold purpose. In the first place, it has given employment to Negroes who are dramatically inclined. In the second place, it has encouraged the development of talent.

The 120 years of Negro drama have seen many changes and experiences in the constantly shifting scenes that have altered the lives of Negroes. Despite vicissitudes, definite advancements have been made, and the drama of the Negro today, while it may not reflect Negro life in its entirety, is, nevertheless, a cultural contribution to the field of drama.

B. CONCLUSIONS

Drama of the Negro has been divided into eight distinct periods of developments. This study has considered: (a) the backgrounds of Negro drama; (b) the efforts of the African Players of the 1820's; (c) minstrelsy; (d) the transitional period; (e) the period of Negro authorship; (f) the period of white authorship of Negro themes; (g) the Federal theatre movement; and (h) the period of the allied arts, dancing and music, respectively.

I. It has been shown in this dissertation that the Negro is, by nature, dramatic. The misery and tragedy experienced by the Negro has served as a background for his drama, and has motivated, to a certain extent, the facile display of his feelings and emotions.

II. During the 1820's a company of African players made commendable showings with their productions of classical drama. Their interpretation of classical plays aroused interest and favorable comment in New York City.

III. Aside from the production of classical plays mentioned above, minstrelsy was the prevailing form of Negro entertainment throughout the nineteenth century. It originated on southern plantations, and later found expression in organized minstrel shows.

IV. During the last decade of the nineteenth century, and the first decade of the twentieth, a different kind of entertainment began to be offered. This new entertainment consisted of clever songs and light comedy.

V. Between 1917 and 1935, plays by Negro writers became more and more numerous. Negro playwrights weakened their drama, however, because of too much sensationalism and propaganda. "Sugar Cane," by Frank Wilson, and "Mulatto," by Langston Hughes, are definite examples.

VI. In 1921, there was a revival of musical comedy, which was very popular during the remainder of the decade. "Shuffle Along," and "Running Wild," by Miller and Lyle, and "The Black Birds," by Lew Leslie, gave evidences of artistic entertainment in musical comedy.

VII. From 1909, through 1937, the white playwright returned to Negro themes and devoted themselves to the more serious aspects of those themes. Edward Sheldon was the first to concern himself with the new themes. Sheldon was followed by Eugene O'Neill, Paul Green and other playwrights.

VIII. The Federal Theatre movement which began in 1935, has made praiseworthy showings in regard to the writing and production of Negro drama. This Federal unit has produced several worthwhile, and commendable plays. The best known of these productions have been "Haiti," "Turpentine," "Dr. Beck," "Macbeth," "Case of Philip Lawrence," and "Swing It."

IX. The Negro has been warmly received on the concert stage. For instance, Paul Robeson, Roland Hayes, Clarence Cameron White, Clarence Muse, and Marion Anderson have been welcomed by concert lovers.

X. The Negro has become recognized as a creator of dances. Dances of Negro origin have been fea-

SUMMARY AND CONCLUSIONS

tured in white productions, with Negroes doing the steps. The most popular of these dances have been "The Charleston," "The Lindy Hop," and "The Big Apple."

XI. White producers and playwrights have commercialized Negro talent, and have gradually taken over, as their own, certain songs and dances that originated with Negroes. As soon as certain dances and songs become common, officials of stage and screen send agents into Negro locale to discover whether or not the new amusement has any commercial value.

XII. Because of racial prejudice, the Negro has been unable to make an appreciable showing on either moving picture or radio programs. Sponsors who have put Negroes on their programs have been threatened with boycott propaganda.

XIII. The 120 years of Negro drama have seen many changes and experiences in the constantly shifting scenes that have altered the lives of Negroes. Despite vicissitudes, definite advancements have been made, and the drama of the Negro today, while it may not reflect Negro life in its entirety, is nevertheless, a cultural contribution to the field of drama.

BIBLIOGRAPHY

BOOKS

1. Bond, F. W., *Speech Construction*. Boston: The Christopher Publishing House, 1936. pp. 82-83.
2. Bradford, Roark, *John Henry*. New York: Harper and Brothers, 1931. pp. 19-60.
3. Brawley, B. J., *The Negro Genius*. New York: Dodd, Meade and Company, 1937. "Drama and Stage from 1916 to 1936," Chapter X, pp. 320-360.
4. Cunard, Nancy, *Negro Anthology*. London: Wishart and Co., 1934. pp. 320-355.
5. Cubberley, E. P., *Public Education in the United States*. Boston and New York: Houghton Mifflin Company, 1919. pp. 431-442.
6. Douglas, Frederick, *Life and Times*. New York: Harper and Brothers, 1892, pp. 415-490.
7. Dow, G. S., *Society and Its Problems*. New York: Thos. Crowell Co., 1920, pp. 185-229.
8. DuBois, W. E. B., *Souls of Black Folk*. Chicago: A. C. McClerg and Company, 1928. pp. 5-9.
9. Fenner, Thos., *Religious Folk Songs of the Negro*. Hampton: Hampton Inst., 1909. pp. 9-70.
10. Hutton, Laurence, *Curiosities of the Stage*. New York: Harper and Brothers, 1891. pp. 270-320.
11. Johnson, C. S., *The Negro in American Civilization*. New York: Henry Holt and Co., 1930. pp. 53-72.
12. Johnson, J. W., *Black Manhattan*. New York: Alfred Knopf, 1930. pp. 115-188.
13. Johnson, J. W., *Along This Way*. New York: The Viking Press, 1935. pp. 60-110.
14. Locke, Alain, *The New Negro*. New York: Albert and Charles Boni, 1925. "Drama of Negro Life," Chapter X, pp. 78-80.
15. Loggins, Vernon, *The Negro Author*. New York: Columbia University, 1930. pp. 52-121.

BIBLIOGRAPHY

16. Matthews, Chas., *Sketches of Celebrated Trips to America*. London: 1861. pp. 11-28.
17. Odell, G. C., *Annals of the Stage*. New York: Columbia University, 1928. Vol. III, p. 70.
18. Odum, H. W., *Negro Workaday Songs*. Chapel Hill: University of North Carolina, 1926. pp. 5-27.
19. Robeson, I. C., *Paul Robeson, Negro*. London: Victor Gallancy, 1930. pp. 30-109.
20. Rowland, Mabel, *Bert Williams, Son of Laughter*. London: English Crafter, 1923. pp. 112-122.
21. Sutherland, E. N., *Criminology*. Philadelphia: Lippincott, 1924. p. 241.
22. Van Vechten, Carl, *Nigger Heaven*. New York: The Viking Press, 1926. pp. 1-220.
23. Washington, B. T., *Up from Slavery*. New York: A. L. Burt and Co., 1900. pp. 20-156.
24. Wheatley, Phyllis, *Poems on Various Subjects*. New York: Thomas and Thomas, 1806.
25. Work, N. H., *The Negro Year Book*. Tuskegee, Ala.: Tuskegee Institute, 1931. pp. 115-119.

PUBLISHED PLAYS

1. Aiken, Geo. L., *Uncle Tom's Cabin*. New York: The Macmillan Co., 1922.
2. Anonymous, *Star of Emancipation*. Boston: Emancipation Society, 1841.
3. Basshe, Em Jo, *Earth*. New York: The McCaulay Company, 1927.
4. Bronwell, J. C., *Mississippi Rain*. New York: Samuel French, Inc., 1931.
5. Bradford, Roark, *How Come Christmas*. New York: London, Harper Bros., 1934.
6. Clark, B., *The American Scene*. D. Appleton and Co., N. Y., 1922.
7. Connelly, M. C., *The Green Pastures*. New York: Farrar and Rinehart, Inc., 1929.
8. Culbertson, E. H., *Goat Alley*. Cincinnati: Stewart Kidd Co., 1922.

9. Edmonds, Randolph, *Shades and Shadows*. Boston: Meadows Publishing Company, 1935. (Six Plays for a Negro Theatre.)

10. Green, Paul, *Plays of Negro Life*. New York: Samuel French, Inc., 1933.

11. Gale, B., *The Hand of Fate*. Nashville: A. M. S. Sunday School Union, 1919.

12. Heyward, Du Bose and Dorothy, *Mamba's Daughter*, N. Y., 1939.

13. Heyward, Du Bose and Dorothy, *Porgy*. Garden City: Doubleday, Doran & Co., 1928.

14. Heyward, Du Bose, *Brass Ankle*. New York: Farrar and Rinehart, 1931.

15. Hughes, L., *Scottsboro Limited*. New York: The Golden Stair Press, 1932.

16. Lawson, Hilda J., *The Negro in American Drama*, an unpublished thesis, The University of Illinois, 1939.

17. Locke, Alain, *Plays of Negro Life*. New York: Harper and Brothers, 1927.

18. Mayorga, Margaret, *Representative One-Act Plays*. Boston: Little, Brown and Co.

19. Meyer, A. N., *Black Souls*. New Bedford: Reynolds Press, 1932.

20. *New List of Negro Plays*. National Service Bureau, Federal Theatre Project.

21. O'Neill, E. *All God's Chillun Got Wings*, American Mercury, 1924.

22. O'Neill, E., Plays: *The Emperor Jones, Gold, The Dreamy Kid*. New York: Boni and Liveright, 1925.

23. Peters, Paul and Sklar, George, *Stevedore*. New York: Covici Friede, 1934.

24. Raphall, Samson, *White Man*. New York: Samuel French, 1935.

25. Richardson, Willis, and Mae Miller, *Negro History in Negro Plays*. Washington: The Associated Publishers, 1927.

26. Richardson, Willis, *Plays and Pageants from the Life of the Negro*. Washington: The Associated Publishers, 1930.

27. Séjour, Victor, *André Geard*, Drame, Paris.

28. Shay, F., *Contemporary One-Act Plays*. New York: Stewart Kidd Co., 1922.

BIBLIOGRAPHY

29. Stowe, H. B., *The Christian Slave.* Boston: Phillips, Sampson and Company, 1855.
30. Shakespeare, William, *Othello.* New York: American Book Co., 1879.
31. Sheldon, E. B., *The Nigger.* New York: The Macmillan Co., 1910.
32. Southerne, Thos., *Oroonoko.* London: 1776.
33. Tanner, Wm., *The Birth of Freedom.* Dayton, Ohio, 1919.
34. Torrence, F. R., *Granny Maumee, The Rider of Dreams, Simon the Cyrenian.* New York: The Macmillan Co., 1917.
35. Ware, Alice H., *Like a Flame.* New York: Theatre League, 1938.
36. Ware, Alice H., *Mighty Wind a-Blowin'.* New York: New Theatre League, 1936.
37. Wexley, John, *They Shall Not Die.* New York: Alfred A. Knopf, 1930.
38. Yates, Elizabeth H., *The Slave.* Philadelphia Publishing Co., 1926.

UNPUBLISHED PLAYS

1. Adams, C. L., *Potee's Gal.*
2. Anderson, Harold, *Smell the Sweet Savior.*
3. Anonymous, *The Second Coming, The Marriage of Cana, Blue and the Gray.*
4. Anonymous, *Roll Sweet Chariot.*
5. Anonymous, *Police System, The Problem of Race.*
6. Anonymous, *Come Along Mandy.*
7. Anonymous, *Brown Buddies.*
8. Bernard, George, *Androcles and the Lion.*
9. Bond, F. W., *Family Affair.*
10. Bryant, George, *The Second Coming.*
11. Brown, John, *Ossawatomie Brown.*
12. Brown, W. Wells, *Experience, Escape, Life at the South.*
13. Childres, Alvin, *Hell's Alley.*
14. Culbertson, Ernest, *Rachey.*
15. Chorpenning, Charlotte, *Little Black Sambo and the Tigers.*

16. Donald, Heywood, *Old Man Satan.*
17. DuBois, William, *Haiti.*
18. Fisher, Rudolph, *Conjure Man Dies.*
19. Gale, Beresford, *Hand of Fate.*
20. Gold, Michael, *Hoboken Blues.*
21. Hamilton, Harry and Foster, Norman, *Savage Rhythm.*
22. Handy, W. C. and Johnson, R., *Memory Lane.*
23. Harris, Bernice, *His Jewels.*
24. Heywood, Donald, *How Come, Lawd?*
25. Hughes, Langston, *Mullatto, Don't You Want to be Free?, Little Ham, Troubled Island.*
26. Jefferson, Joseph, *The Octoroon.*
27. Johnson, J. W., *A Trip to Coontown.*
28. Johnson, Hall, *Run Little Chillun.*
29. Jones, Earl Aubrey, *Port of No Where.*
30. Leslie, Lew, *Black Birds of 1939.*
31. MacEntee, George, *The Case of Philip Lawrence.*
32. McGowan, John, *Singing the Blues.*
33. Millen, James K., *Never No More.*
34. Nicholson, Kenyon, *Sailor Beware.*
35. Putnam, Mary, *Tragedy of Errors.*
36. Raphaelson, Samson, *White Man.*
38. Ship, Jess A., *In Dehomey; Mr. Lode of Kole.*
39. Smith, J. A., *Turpentine.*
40. Thurman, Wallace and Rapp, J., *Harlem.*
41. Trowbridge, J. T., *Neighbor Jackwood.*
42. Trowbridge, J. T., *Octoroon.*
43. Tutt, Salem Whitney and J. Homer Tutt, *Expresident of Liberia, Mayor of Newton, His Excellency The President, George Washington Bullion Abroad, My People, Darkest Americans, Children of the Sun, Up and Down, Oh Joy, Deep Harlem.*
44. Wilson, Frank, *Sugar Cane.*
45. Wilson, Frank, *Walk Together Chillun.*
46. Ware, Alice H., *Mighty Wind a-Blowin'.*

PERIODICAL REFERENCES

1. Andrews, C. B., Ira Aldridge. *Crisis* (October, 1935), p. 26.

BIBLIOGRAPHY

2. Anonymous, Negro Drama. *The Nation,* Vol. 124, No. 3217 (March 2, 1927), pp. 242-243.
3. Anonymous, Drama. *Time* (November 1, 1935), p. 58.
4. Anonymous, A Negro Theatre. *Theatre Arts Monthly* (December, 1927), pp. 483-491.
5. Anonymous, Who Invented Jazz? *Collier's Weekly* (January 3, 1925), p. 22.
6. Anonymous, *Genius of Universal Emancipation,* Vol. XI, p. 497.
7. Brawley, B. J., The Negro Literary Renaissance, *Southern Workman* (April, 1927), pp. 30-32.
8. Brown, Sterling, Negro Character as Seen through White Authors. *Journal of Negro Education* (April, 1933), pp. 42-49.
9. Brown, Sterling, Roland Hayes. *Opportunity* (June, 1925), pp. 16-17.
10. Chapin, E., Where Jazz Comes From. *Popular Mechanics* (January, 1926), p. 97.
11. Clime, Julia, Rise of the American Stage Negro. *Drama Magazine* (January, 1931), pp. 56-57.
12. Dett, R. N., The Emancipation of Negro Music. *Southern Workman* (April, 1918), p. 172.
13. Edmonds, Randolph, Some Reflections on the Negro in American Drama. *Opportunity* (October, 1930), pp. 303-305.
14. Gregory, Montgomery, The Negro Actor. *The New Republic* (November 16, 1921), pp. 523-526.
15. Harrison, Hubert, The Significance of Lula Belle. *Opportunity* (May, 1926), p. 228.
16. Harrison, B. B., Jes Like a Natchel Man. *Christian Herald* (March, 1935), p. 19.
17. Hughes, Langston, The Negro Artist and the Racial Mountain. *The Nation* (June 23, 1926), p. 692.
18. Krutch, J. W., Black Ecstasy. *The Nation* (October 26, 1927).
19. Johnson, C. S., Ira Aldridge. *Opportunity* (March, 1925), p. 6.
20. Locke, Alain, Toward a Critique of Negro Music. *Crisis* (November, 1934), p. 60.
21. Nathan, C. J., *The American Mercury* (July, 1924), p. 36.

THE NEGRO AND THE DRAMA

22. Smith, Morgan, The Negro as Artist. *The Radical,*
    Vol. II, 1867, pp. 27-31.
23. Tichemor, G., Colored Lines. *Theatre Arts Monthly*
    (January, 1930), pp. 485-490.
24. Van Vechten, Carl, Beginning of Negro Drama. *Literary Digest* (May 1, 1914), p. 1114.
25. Young, Stark, Negro Material in the Theatre. *The New Republic* (May 11, 1927), p. 92.

INDEX

A

Adams, C. L., his "Potee's Gal," 178

Allen, Richard, pastoral influences of, 6-7

Anderson, Eddie "Rochester," in "Man About Town," 103

Anderson, Marian, contralto, 57

Angus, Bernie, "Brown Sugar" of, 91

Antony, Emmett, dramatic appearance of, 54

Anti-slavery drama, 23

B

Baker, Josephine, as dancer, 142

Barnum, P. T., associated with minstrelsy, 18

Banting, John, a critic of Negro dancing, 143

Barrymore, Ethel, tribute to Rose McClendon, 84

Basshe, Em Jo, "Earth," author of, 81-82

Beavers, Louise, as actress, 157-58

Belcher, Fannin S., his organization and objectives, 131-32

Belasco, David, as critic, 64; as producer, 80-81

Bickerstaffe, Isaac, in "Mungo," 31-32

Blake, Clinton L., his efforts, 133

Blair, Mary, talented actress, 73

Bledsoe, Jules, as actor, 57-8, 76

"Bojangles," see Robinson, Bill

Bond, F. W., "Family Affair," 189

Bowes, Major, his radio program, 100

Brach, Frances, her start, 101

Brown, Ada, "Queen of Blues," 158; as actress, 176

Brown, Ralph, ecstatic capers, 99

Brown, Wm. Wells, drama of, 25-26

Bryant, Willie, his acting, 95

C

Calloway, Cab, band of, 140-141; achievements, 145-146

Carter, Jack, as actor in "MacBeth," 170

Castle, Vernon, impression of Negro dances, 138

Callendar, Charles, associated with minstrelsy, 18

Churches, influence and expenditure of, 12-13

Clough, Inez, as actress, 66-67

Comedy, light, 175

Connley, Marcus, "Green Pastures," 64

Conner, E. S., actor and reporter, 17

Cooper, Ralph, screen actor, 159

Comathiere, A. B., as actor, 177-178, 192

Cole, Bob, as song writer, 39-41

Crummell, Alexander, preacher, 30

Dance and jazz, a folk art contribution, 138

209

INDEX

D

Dawson, William L., symphony of, 59

Dietz, Howard, "At Home Abroad," 90

Donoghue, Dennis, his "Legal Murder," 113-114

Douglas, Frederick, as editor and abolitionist, 8-9

Drama, recent Negro, 108; problems of, 182

DuBois, W., as author of "Haiti," 172

Dunbar, Paul Laurence, as poet, 39

E

Edmonds, Randolph, his dramatic awakening, 123-128; at Dillard University, 136

Enoch, Frederick, as critic of drama, 123

Evanti, Lillian, in operatic circles of Europe, 56

F

"Fetchit, Stepin," ranking Negro screen actor, 158

Fisher, Rudolph, his "Walls of Jericho," 118

Forest, Thomas, comic opera of, 20

G

Graves, Aubrey, as critic, 84

Gilpin, Charles, as actor, 64; speaks to Cleveland amateurs, 129

H

Hammon, Jupiter, poetry of, 2-3

Handy, W. C., father of "Blues," 43-44

Hackley, Azalia, success on concert stage, 56

Hall, Adelaide, as actress in "Brown Buddies," 176

Hamilton, Harry, "Savage Rhythm," 97

Harlem, actors of, perform in Canada, 106

Harris, Connie, in a western production, 160

Harris, Edna Mae, in "The Spirit of Youth," 161

Harrison, Richard B., "Green Pastures," actor in, 91-93

Hayes, Roland, tenor, 57

Hedgeman, Merrit, at Brooklyn Academy of Music, 56

Hernandez, Juano, as actor, 178

Henderson, Fletcher, ragtime entertainment of, 146; as Blues critic, 148

Heyward, DuBose, as dramatist, 82-84; 95-96; as reviewer, 105

Heywood, Donald, as writer and producer, 176

Hicks, Charles, organizer of Georgia minstrels, 19

Higgins, Billie, player, 90

Hill, Abraham, "Hell's Half Acre," of, 189

Hill, Leslie P., "Jethro" of, 189

Holdship, Alice, "Mighty Wind a-Blowin' " of, 184

Huey, Richard, as producer, 106; in "Three Men on a Horse," 161

Hughes, Langston, as dramatist, 114

Hughes, Revella, as actress, 121

Hurst, Fannie, her popular attitude, 157

Hurston, Zora Neale, mimicry, 16

Hutton, Laurence, critic, 32

I

Independent effort, 44

Ingram, Rex, as actor, 92, 172

Irvin, May, features songs of, 39

210

INDEX

J

James, Gee Gee, her stage appearance, 102

Jackson, Blyden, his organization, 135-136

Jackson, Sam, burlesque reputation, 44

Jeffries, Herbert, as actor, 160

Jefferson, Joseph, as producer, 28

Johnson, James Weldon, as dramatic writer, 39-41

Johnson, Georgia, her "Frederick Douglas," 188-189

Johnson, Hall, as dramatist, 144, 174

Johnson, J. R., as composer, 177

Johnson, Lew, organizer of minstrel company, 19

Johnson, J. Rosamond, his chair, 98

Jones, Aubrey, "Port of Nowhere," 190

Jones, Sissiereta, as "Black Patti," 47

Jonson, Ben, writer, 33, 127

K

Kersands, William, co-creator of jazz, 19

King, Wallace, co-creator of jazz, 19

Kirk, Andy, orchestra of, 152

Kirkpatrick, Sidney, talent of, 42

Kober, Arthur, "Having a Wonderful Time," 131

Koster and Bial, Directors, 48

L

Layton, John, T., interest of, in dramatic music, 56

Leacock, John, "The Fall of British Tyranny," 20

Leslie, Lew, his rhapsodic review, 98; his "Blackbirds," 84, 180, 181

Lèvinson, Andre, impression of Negro dancing, 141-142

Lillard, J. A., international actor, 101

Little Theatre movement, 122

Lunceford, Jimmie, "swing" orchestra of, 102, 152

M

Mackye, Steele, "A Fool's Errand," 28

Marcus, Frank D., stage technique of, 84

Marlowe, Christopher, his plays, 135

Matheus, John F., his "Ti Yette," 112; "Cruiter," 193

McClendon, Rose, as actress, 76, 84

McCoo, Edward, his "Ethiopia at the Bar of Justice," 39

McKinney, Maurice, portrayal cf "Rev. Green," 193

McKinney, Nina Mae, first Negro girl to pass screen test, 158

"Mikado, Hot," rearranged and produced, 99-101

Middleton, George, his thoughts in the theme of plays, 88

Miller, G. C., talent of, 42

Mills, Florence, as dancer, 142; theatrical career, 181

Mitchell, Abbie, her start to fame, 47; as actress, 76

Morean, Chas. C., African company of, 21-22

Moss, Carlton, as script writer, 128-129; dramalogues of, 163

211

INDEX

INDEX